CHRISTIAN EDUCATION FOR SOCIALLY HANDICAPPED CHILDREN AND YOUTH

*

*A Manual for Chaplains and Teachers
of Persons Under Custody*

ELEANOR EBERSOLE

Published for The Cooperative Publication Association by
UNITED CHURCH PRESS
PHILADELPHIA   BOSTON

Library of Congress Catalog Card Number 64-25579

Contents

Acknowledgments

MANY PEOPLE have contributed to this manual. It was conceived and planned by a subcommittee of the Committee on Christian Education of Exceptional Persons of the National Council of Churches. The original outline was written by Phyllis Maramarco. The members of the subcommittee who contributed to the manual are: Oliver B. Gordon, chairman; T. C. Cooke; John C. Gould; Phyllis Maramarco (now deceased); Melvin L. Oehrtman; Harold G. Nixon; Grace Pelon; Robert L. Potts; Virginia Stafford; Louise N. Sutton; J. B. Wilson; and J. Blaine Fister, staff adviser.

Selected readers' comments have been exceedingly valuable and led to worthwhile additions and special emphases. These persons include: Jackson R. Day, M.D.; Charles B. Grimm; Malcolm D. Maccubbin; Oren N. Reneau; Robert H. Scott; Virgil L. Sprunger; and William D. Tyndall.

Appreciation is expressed to those who have contributed directly to the author's perception of the educational, psychological, spiritual, and physical needs of persons. Many of these people have not read the manual or have read only portions of it. Included in this group are professors at Teachers College of Columbia University, Hartford Seminary Foundation, and Union Theological Seminary; Richard A. Crandall, M.D.; Marshall W. House, D.O.; and my husband, Jay F. Ebersole, with whom I share in Christian ministry. Special appreciation is extended also to Ethel Mecum, superintendent, Long Lane School, Middletown, Connecticut, and to William C. Adamson, M.D., for permission to use his revision of the 1958 statement of objectives of religious education by the National Council of Churches.

ELEANOR EBERSOLE

1 / The Purpose of the Manual

❋

THESE ARE wonderful, exploding, terrifying, and changing days in which we live. While many islands of stable, routine life remain, much of American society is participating in the beginnings of a new age or resisting its eventuality.

THE PREDICAMENT OF THE SOCIALLY HANDICAPPED

Caught in the changing patterns of life and social class structure are thousands of children and youth. They are unable to find a place satisfying to themselves and to society. They see the double standards of adult lives; their homes are often unstable; the routines and words of the church seem irrelevant; they know hopelessness in school, in unemployment, and in racial discrimination.

Those caught in the deprived urban culture feel the impossibility of ever attaining the affluent life of television commercials. Some learn to hate all adults whom they hold responsible for their predicament. Some become mentally ill with unresolved conflicts. Some find pleasure and excitement wherever they can—theft, fighting, sex. They rebel and they hate. The world they know, the feelings they experience cannot be covered up.

The acting out of these feelings may start anywhere. Overt trouble may begin at school where no one has cared who they are inside; it may start in a middle-class broken

5

home or with parents who impose intolerable religious or social restrictions which leave no room for growth as a person of integrity. It may start with fighting the cultural trap of the inner city. The youngsters begin to drop out of school, to commit sexual offenses, to steal.

Finally when society can no longer tolerate their anti-social behavior, the youth encounter the law. Some are fortunate enough to be given competent guidance and professional therapy in their own community and find a new life within society. Others are declared "delinquent" by the courts and are institutionalized where they may receive help, but many travel the road in and out of various institutions until their crimes against society become so persistent that they must be placed permanently under custody.

THE NEED

These are the socially handicapped children and youth. Their behavior patterns are a major handicap to them. Their adaptation to the environment with which they have been confronted prevents them from finding fulfillment of their lives in ways which are acceptable to society. Their values are not the values of those in control of existing community activities or of those who make the laws. They are in need of help—the best help which science and the Christian community can give to them. Such help is available, but the process is slow, the trained personnel is limited, the expense is great, and the results are not guaranteed.

This manual will serve as a guide for chaplains and teachers who accept the challenge of making religion meaningful and helpful to the children and youth who find their predicament in society more than they can tolerate. It is Jesus, the friend of sinners and outcasts, who sets the example. It is he who ate with Zacchaeus, talked with the Samaritans, loved the misfits, and forgave the thief beside him on a cross, who leads the teacher in ways of acceptance

6

and of respect for persons with problems. Through Christ's presence in the Christian community it is still possible to create appropriate ways of meeting the needs of these troubled youngsters and of leading them out of their present predicament. Participating in such an educational mission of the church demands of the teacher personal spiritual maturity, a spirit of adventure, a willingness to learn new skills, and a knowledge that ultimately it is God who heals and gives new life.

THE MANUAL

Zeal and faith are not enough in planning for the Christian education of socially troubled children and youth. A great deal of knowledge and skill are also essential. The manual is intended primarily for lay teachers of Christian education and for Christian educators beginning work with socially handicapped youngsters in institutional situations. Its purpose is to help teachers understand the nature of the children they teach, to have a knowledge of some appropriate teaching procedures, and to be familiar with institutional procedures and regulations.

The Contents will serve as a guide to those who are interested in particular aspects of the church's ministry of Christian education to socially handicapped children and youth. Readers who wish to go beyond the nontechnical survey materials of this manual are encouraged to read widely in the books listed in the annotated Bibliography.

The youngsters described here are primarily older-elementary and teen-age children. The constituency of institutions for delinquents varies greatly. Many state institutions must accept any one committed to them by the courts. In an educational program it is wise to separate younger and older children because of their differing educational skills, interests, and problems. It also seems wise to provide different groups for youth who wish to discuss religious ideas and those who respond better to a more physically active learning situation. In this manual emphasis is placed on concrete experiences and concepts in discussions and in all other activities. While many of the youth are normal or above in intelligence, their educational progress has usually been limited by their inability to get along in school. This educational retardation needs to be recognized.

Though written especially for teachers in institutional situations, the manual contains descriptions of socially handicapped children and youth and many suggestions of ways of working with them that are appropriate for a local church or community program. In such cases parents should certainly be considered as coplanners and assistants in the program. Chapter 2 and the Bibliography deal specifically with the relationship between the local church and the community and the socially handicapped youngster.

THE CHOICE OF TITLE

The term socially handicapped is used to encompass the vast and subtle problems of children and youth who are at odds with society for any of a variety of reasons suggested in this manual. The problems of these children and youth have led to actions which are intolerable to society, and thus to placement in custody for the protection of both the child or youth and society. Regardless of the cause of the youngster's actions, or even the rightness of them, society through its courts has decided that these actions cannot be tolerated. His patterns of action have thus become a handicap to him. His social behavior prevents him from functioning within an unrestricted society. Ultimately it is the action of the youngster which determines his being placed under custody; thus he might be described as handicapped by his social behavior, the cause of which may or may not be known.

8

2 / The Socially Handicapped in Church and Community

He told them a parable also: "No one tears a piece from a new garment and puts it upon an old garment; if he does he will tear the new, and the piece from the new will not match the old."—LUKE 5:36

SOCIETY IS CHANGING RAPIDLY. A new age is stirring. It is reported that by 1965 half of the population of the United States will be under twenty-five years of age. Urban areas will extend over major portions of the Atlantic and Pacific coastlines. Stopgap measures for meeting the spiritual, educational, social, and occupational needs of children and youth are not adequate to the increasing challenge. They have not been adequate in the past, especially in urban areas. "Urban ferment," "racial injustice," "suburban complacency," and "technological advance" are abstract and inadequate generalizations to express the shifting, rumbling, hurtling progress of civilization into a new age.

Church and community institutions will be new. They are becoming new where they respond with the use of their power to support justice and functional change for the good of all. The church, as we know it, will either petrify in stagnation or join in the new age with openness, spiritual power, and leadership. The power of Christianity lies in the knowledge that the historical act of God's revelation in

9

Jesus Christ is constantly made contemporary through his living Spirit. Spirit-filled Christians witnessing boldly may help shape the new world.

Children and youth are particularly vulnerable to social change and instability in families, to the rigid holding actions of prejudice and established institutions, and to the lack of provision for them in the working world. The number of youngsters in rebellion, already judged delinquent, will continue to increase unless society and the church in society function more adequately in offering help for personal problems and in working to alleviate intolerable pressures which fester into rebellion, hatred, and despair. This means an attack on fundamental attitudes and values of society which may be divisive and demoralizing. "New garments," new societal attitudes and experiments, and new persons are needed.

There is knowledge with which to work. Religion, science, medicine, politics, economics are contributing increasingly greater understanding about the forces at work in society and the interaction of personality within the total. This knowledge is essential background for the Christian educator who wishes to participate in the great experiment of the Christian community at work in a new world. A Bible in hand and good intentions will not solve the problems of thousands, actually millions, of youth grappling with pressures unknown twenty years ago. If the church is not to be a series of isolated irrelevant islands— pharisees of the 60's—it must participate in the formation of tomorrow as leader and goalsetter. The Bibliography has been selected for the purpose of broadening the Christian educator's understanding of the total picture of services to the socially handicapped.

"Cooperation" is the key word to the work of the church in the community. Work must begin with meeting the needs of all persons before hatreds and rebellion develop. The sore spots of society must be dealt with critically and constantly. Those youngsters already troubled in their relationships with society need help through (1) detecting their problems as early as possible, (2) providing immediate remedial help in the community, (3) aiding the delinquent youngsters on probation in the community, (4) offering spiritual support and Christian nurture while a delinquent is in custody, and (5) aiding in the reintegration of institutionalized youth into the community upon their return. All the agencies of society must work together, each contributing its particular framework and values. The remainder of this chapter deals with aspects of the work of the church and community with the socially handicapped youngsters.

PREVENTING SOCIAL HANDICAPS

Community planning is basic in meeting the needs of all children and youth. This cooperative venture involves the parents, schools, churches, service agencies, scouting, YMCA, and so on. It involves reaching out to youngsters who do not normally find their way to social or recreation groups. These neglected "loners" are often the ones most in need of positive social experiences and the opportunity to relate happily to a mature adult. School dropouts need to be reached. Guidance must be offered to children of the increasing number of divorced parents. Ghettos formed under pressure of cultural and racial prejudice must be eliminated.

In small cities and towns one informal way to determine whether or not the needs of children and youth are being adequately met is "keeping an ear to the ground." What do the youth complain about consistently? Do they moan about nothing to do? How high is the dropout rate from school? Are there gangs of youngsters hanging around corners? How high is the rate of juvenile crime? What facilities are offered for the care of children of working mothers? What about open housing?

11

Church leaders who are sensitive to the feelings and problems of persons both within the church and in the community soon become aware of the needs of persons which are not being met. Some churches have taken action to meet needs in the following manner:

» providing recreation and meeting-place facilities for youth
» offering out-of-school tutoring and provision for study space if needed
» holding vocational planning programs
» encouraging mature adults to take personal interest in individual children and youth facing problems of enormity
» critically evaluating church school and youth programs to find who is missing and why
» providing good Christian foster homes in adequate numbers (a very practical and significant contribution)
» providing child-care programs which offer preschool learning experiences
» making mature adults available for informal conversations
» welcoming all persons through positive outreach into the community
» supporting community action in any area of need— open housing, youth recreation, new schools, and so on.

Preventing social handicaps in the massive metropolitan areas is a staggering proposition. Only through cooperative movements with strong leadership committed to the total good of society can rapid change, subcultures, prejudices, and anonymity be directed toward the betterment of social conditions. Church leaders now have available current magazine articles and books containing considerable critical material about urban problems which will be helpful in planning Christian education strategy.

Early Detection of Rebellion and Hate

Detecting potential social handicaps is a cooperative venture. Parents, schoolteachers, pastors, storekeepers, all have a responsibility to observe the youngster who is beginning to manifest antisocial behavior. Shrugging shoulders and looking the other way when children destroy property or jump on top of parked cars may be an easy way out, but following up the matter to determine who the youngsters are and whether help is needed would be a more responsible action. A word to pastor, scout or local recreation leader might lead to attempts to include the early offender in constructive group activities or, if necessary, to a visit to a child guidance center. Scolding parents is not the answer, nor is ignoring the beginning of trouble.

In the large urban areas detection of rebellion and hate is not difficult. In some neighborhood areas it exists in such volume that it is overwhelming. Cooperative community action in neighborhoods of the city is one road to improving conditions and seeing to it that proper counseling services are available.

Church congregations need to accept responsibility for their community or city. Presently this is not the practice of most churches. If the agencies which serve youth are not adequate, then leadership and finances are obviously necessary. Of what greater use could the resources of the church be put than to help persons with problems find new ways of living in the name of Christ.

Subway, billboard, and newspaper space is used by some communities to advertise services available to any person with a problem. More communities need to take action to see that the social services of the community are well known to those in need.

Four primary sources of social, psychiatric, and health services are available to churches and families[1]:

1. *Community welfare council.* The community welfare council is usually the central planning organization for social and health services, public and private, in a community. Over 500 American cities have a community welfare council or council of social agencies. In some instances the organization goes by another name; if so, this can be secured from the community chest or united fund. In many of the large cities the council maintains an information and referral service that keeps up-to-date information on all social and health resources. Each church should be acquainted with the situation in its own community.

2. *Councils of churches.* There are now over 950 city, county, and state councils of churches in the United States and 2,000 local and state councils of United Church Women. These councils can usually be of help in learning about resources. Twenty-seven of the larger city councils have a staffed social welfare department that works closely with the community welfare council and its information and referral service, if one exists. Some cities that do not have an information and referral service in the social welfare council do have a social welfare department in the council of churches.

3. *The family service society.* In Canada and the United States over three hundred family casework (counseling) agencies are accredited members of the Family Service Association of America.[2] These agencies are accessible to 50 percent of the population of the United States and 23 percent of the population of Canada. Teamwork between churches and these agencies is important; ministers and leading lay workers should become acquainted with the agency supervisors and know how to make referrals.

4. *Public departments.* Churches and their families have access to city, county, and state departments of mental health,

[1] Sheldon L. Rahn, "Community Agencies Can Help," in *International Journal of Religious Education* (February 1962), pp. 20, 46.
[2] 44 East 23rd Street, New York, N. Y. 10010.

14

public health, or welfare, which can give information about agency resources of all kinds. Information about outpatient, psychiatric clinics and inpatient hospital care for mental illness can be obtained from the department of mental health. The county medical society can give names and qualifications of private psychiatrists.

When a needed service is missing. In spite of the progress made in developing social agencies, in some communities services are lacking or are inadequate. When this is the case, the churches can be helpful in getting these services started. The social relations or a similar committee of the church can well initiate action.

The first step is to discover the facts about what exists and what is needed. These can be secured from the welfare council, the council of churches, or the county or state welfare department. From these sources the church may find one or more professional persons who can guide the church in joining forces with other groups to develop public interest.

There are both state and national organizations, private and public, that can often be of help in organizing a new service. The Family Service Association of America recently published a pamphlet "How to Organize a Family Agency." The National Survey Services (sponsored jointly by the Child Welfare League of America, the National Travelers Aid Association, the National Council on Crime and Delinquency, and the Family Service Association of America) is one of several [organizations] that make community surveys to help citizens plan for needed services.

FOR THE DELINQUENT IN THE COMMUNITY

Once a youngster has been apprehended by the law and is placed on probation in the community, the total community has a grave responsibility to provide local services which are adequate for helping him. The church is venturing to a limited extent in cooperative provision for spiritual and material support of these youngsters. The following are suggestive ways in which the churches are now working with delinquent youth:

1. Within the churches there are persons who are concerned with developing a better understanding of youth on the part of adults and breaking down the old stereotypes about them. Pastors and mature lay leaders are recognizing the need for personal acceptance and support of "difficult" youth. Judgment has been made by the court; trust and respect are needed from the church. Many churches are extending to troubled youth and their families social, spiritual, and financial support according to their needs. The financial support is often accomplished through an anonymous "pastor's fund."

2. Some cities have a volunteer corps of pastors and laymen who act as chaplains or friends of delinquent youth, going to court with them and offering whatever help is needed during their probationary period. This extension of spiritual and material concern is offered to all youth who come before the court.

3. Personal counseling with individual youngsters is made available in the church where this is not being done by a casework agency under direction of the court. Help is offered to the youngster in finding new activities and friends to replace the environment which contributed to antisocial behavior. Tutoring services are offered to the educationally retarded.

4. Occasionally workshops in the processes of group work and guidance techniques are offered to church leaders. This skill is of considerable value in integrating "delinquent" youth into church school programs in a way beneficial to all. Pastors who have received clinical training often work individually with their youth leaders. Some training in group work is available through public institutions. The State of Michigan offers in-service training to group counselors working within institutions for persons under custody.

5. Denominational support of special ministries is given to urban parish centers for the culturally and socially disadvantaged. The cost of professional staff, facilities, and materials far exceeds the financial resources available in the local parish. Two books in the Bibliography describe attempts at meeting the needs of delinquents within the urban situation: *Light the Dark Streets* by C. Kilmer Myers, and *Children Who Hate* by Fritz Redl and David Wineman.

For the Delinquent Under Custody in an Institution

Experience has shown that work with youngsters in custody is best done interdenominationally. Generally the council of churches on a state level shares in the selection of resident chaplains in state institutions. Private institutions may turn to state councils of churches for recommendations of qualified persons for chaplaincy positions. Another approach is for local councils of churches or groups of ministers to offer voluntary chaplaincy services. Also local pastors of particular individual youngsters may visit to give the sacraments, offer religious counseling, and make preparation for confirmation. Pastors living at considerable distance from the institution tend to work through the resident chaplain or the ministerial group related to the institution.

Christian education is also best planned and carried out through interdenominational channels. Where a resident chaplain is in charge of the religious program, he will probably be directly responsible for Christian education programs. In other cases local or state councils of churches may plan, support, and staff Christian education programs in coordination with a staff member of the institution. Persons aware of the lack of Christian education for youngsters in a particular institution may initiate action through an appropriate interdenominational group.

Local churches near residential institutions for delinquent youngsters provide helpful services which demonstrate to these youngsters that the church cares and that as persons they are not hopelessly cut off from society. In all cases the institution has the ultimate authority in determining program. Some institutions prefer all work with children and youth to be done on the campus of the institution. Others feel interaction with the community prepares the road back to the community when the youngster is ready. Of course no action by the local church should be taken without the knowledge and cooperation of the institutional staff. The following services by churches near institutions have proven to be helpful:

» aiding in the provision of Christian foster homes, if needed, when youngsters are ready to leave the institution

» providing teachers for the institutional Christian education program

» offering talents and skills of lay members of churches to work with staff personnel

» working for community acceptance of youngsters under custody as individuals and not as "institution kids" and encouraging the expression of these attitudes in the community's relationships with the institution

» organizing community baseball teams to play the institutional team

» "adopting" a youngster recommended by the institution: occasionally inviting the youngster to spend Sunday with the family, remembering birthdays, and visiting on visiting days.

The church community as well as the rest of society basically fears the delinquent: "He might marry my daughter!" "She might lead my own daughter astray." "Can I trust him not to pull a knife?" The wall between the institution and the community remains high psychologically in a time when some institutions have removed the physical walls and unlocked the doors. Forgiveness and trust are not easily extended to the antisocial youngster. Yet it is the delinquent who is desperately in need of them. The lack of acceptance and trust on the part of adults may have contributed to his problems initially.

Christians must accept the challenge of meeting the needs of delinquent youth. The challenge is not easy; socially handicapped youngsters are not easy to live with. Yet to deny this ministry is to deny the ministry of Christ.

FACILITATING THE RETURN OF THE DELINQUENT TO SOCIETY

It is generally agreed that the prognosis is poor for a youngster who leaves an institution and returns to the same pressures which contributed to his commitment. The environment to which a youngster returns is very significant. The family, the church, the school, and the community need to understand their contributing roles in the formation of social habits.

When the past environment of a youngster cannot be changed and returning the child or youth seems inadvisable, a new place of residence must be provided. Here the church can help. Good foster homes are again one solution.

When a youngster returns to an environment or enters a new one, spiritual, educational, and material support are needed. Old rejections may rekindle old hatreds. New social group opportunities should be extended so that the youngster will not need to return to the old "gang." It is possible for the church to play a major role in offering the help needed. Often this does happen for youngsters who were already related to a church.

The nonchurch-related youngsters, however—and these youngsters predominate—will be returning without any church to care about them. Whatever Christian experiences they may have had at an institution may be demonstrated to be irrelevant. The old barriers rise. Christians do not really care—enough. Cultural and social gaps (see page 36) rear up again. The church does not really care about persons who do not fit or who are not "our kind of people."

The cooperative approach is again a possible answer. Chaplains of institutions might inform community interdenominational groups about the return of specific youngsters and describe their needs. The council might work toward locating a church where the youngster will be accepted and welcome. In the urban area, city parish workers might be alerted to the youngster's needs. Unless the Christian church, however, in its individual parishes identifies itself with the problems of the urban metropolis, the chances of a delinquent youngster's having the opportunity to continue his spiritual growth under the guidance of mature Christian leadership are very slim.

3 / The Socially Handicapped
Child or Youth

Meet Linda

There was one thing almost everyone said about Linda: "She was always such a nice girl. What happened to her?" Linda had been committed by the court to an institution for "delinquent girls."

Underneath Linda's average appearance and pleasant smile was an adolescent who had been put on probation for stealing cosmetics and clothing, and now was three months pregnant. In Linda's home there was a conflict between her father who refused to let Linda have dates and her mother who slipped Linda money for "little extras." Linda's mother wanted her daughter to be popular but did not know how to help her. Linda's late-night dates were covered up by her mother, and when discovered, were severely punished by her father.

One Saturday night while her father was away on a business trip, Linda was picked up by police in a vacant house with three boys. The court placed Linda in an institution where she could have her baby and begin to face the inner conflicts and rebellion which had led to delinquent behavior.

Meet John

John was defiant and unmanageable in school. His seventh-grade teacher confessed she was relieved the day he

21

"skipped" school. Neither his reading nor arithmetic was up to his grade level. When not in school, he wandered in the neighborhood looking for excitement. John's mother worked in a clothing factory and his own father was unknown, though several men had lived with his mother. John became known to the court authorities as a result of a number of fights and incidents in his neighborhood. In November while John was truant from school, a muffled voice called in a bomb scare. The call was traced to John. An investigation of John's home by a social worker revealed great disorder and filth. The mother admitted her inability to control her son. The court placed John in an institution for rehabilitation and remedial education.

WHO ARE THE SOCIALLY HANDICAPPED?

These simple sketches of John and Linda reflect some of the problems of delinquent children and youth. The sketches do not, however, convey the depth of conflict within the youngster or his family and the complexity of the process of deciding upon appropriate action in the best interests of the child, the parents, and the whole community.

In general it might be said that a child or youth is socially handicapped when he is unable to make adjustments to his life situation in a manner which is acceptable to society. Unacceptable behavior is habitual for some socially handicapped youngsters; for others it is an occasional outburst. This behavior may reflect the values of his friends or it may be an individual reaction to internal or external pressures. The socially handicapped youngster is unable to live comfortably in his total environment. He is handicapped by his inability to adjust, or to cope with life in a way that is approved by adults.

Just what constitutes socially unacceptable behavior? Essentially it is behavior which breaks the rules by which the adult community expects children and youth to live. It is breaking with the expected normal behavior of a particular society. This normbreaking behavior is a matter of degree. Everyone who acts differently from his neighbor is not socially maladjusted. The amount or degree of unacceptable behavior, or normbreaking, is the significant factor. A child who tells a "white lie" in order to escape punishment at home, is not socially maladjusted. This young child may be experimenting in human relationships. He may be testing ways of adjusting in a manner common to most children. In this situation he may be choosing what appears to be a practical way to avoid punishment. After a period of "white lies" he may find them of only limited value.

It is the child who habitually twists information to gain his own ends or to feel superior to others who is on the way toward developing habitual actions which will be a handicap to him. His values are not those of the normal child. In time this pattern of action or adjustment may become a real problem to the youngster. It may cause him difficulty with his friends and may eventually cause him difficulty with a police officer.

When socially unacceptable behavior involves breaking a law it is named "delinquent" behavior. Delinquency is a legal term which indicates that a child has broken a law and has been caught. The term does not define the nature or the severity of the offense. Delinquent behavior may represent the acting out of the problems of a socially handicapped child. It may represent the only possible action to a child, such as stealing food when none is provided by parents, or running away when family pressures or pressures within the self become too severe.

To a youngster, delinquent action may not seem inappropriate; it may be his habitual way of adjusting to the situation in which he lives. Delinquent behavior often represents participation in gang action of peers whose social values differ from those of society. The youngster then is conforming to peer standards rather than adult standards. He is desirous of peer approval rather than the approval of adult society.

MEET TOMMY

Tommy has been moved from one teacher to another, from one school to another, and finally into a special class for retarded children. Tommy is not retarded, but he is "unmanageable" and "disruptive." Outside of school Tommy is also in trouble. Some mothers will not let their boys play with him since he is usually the leader in fights and window-breaking. At home Tommy's parents are "distraught." They finally swallow their pride and ask for help from a family service agency. Will his habitual aggression and defiance become such a handicap to him that he will not grow up as a contributing member of society? The hope that it will not lies in the ability of Tommy, his parents, and professional counselors and therapists to discover the many contributing causes to Tommy's behavior and begin the long process of rehabilitation.

Normbreaking and delinquent behavior are judged according to the degree in which they disrupt society. Seldom is an adolescent committed to an institution or residential school for his first offense, unless this action represents a major threat to the safety of the community and the youngster himself. In this case a psychosis or neurosis is often evident. Emotional disturbances are very much a part of antisocial behavior. Being involved in unruly actions or a petty theft from a variety store does not warrant removal from society. It does warrant guidance by a competent person or child guidance clinic. An accumulation of offenses of more severe nature does indicate the need of positive action for the protection of society and for the sake of the youngster.

Meet Andy

When Andy's mother died early in his life, Andy was placed in the care of an aunt and his father disappeared. Three years later the aunt refused to accept responsibility for him because of a new husband. From that time Andy was moved in and out of a series of foster homes. These moves were necessitated by his uncontrollable behavior. While in the last home he became one of the leaders in a street gang and was placed on probation for several minor offenses. Finally he was caught in a car theft and placed in a residential institution for boys.

Meet Hundreds of Urban Youngsters

A large percentage of delinquent youth in institutions come from the great urban populations of the nation. The ones in this group have special cultural and educational problems. Sometimes their parents are non-English speaking, and have unskilled jobs or are unemployed. Their homes offer little in preparation for school-learning. The children enter school without the early childhood experiences which give meaning to the written word. For many, failure in reading results, discouragement grows, and eventual dropping out of school is the consequence. This pattern of school failure often leads to idleness, street gangs, and rebellion expressed in theft, the use of narcotics, and major crime. Chapter 7 deals in more detail with problems related to school education.

Factors in Social Maladjustment

There is as much danger in generalizing about socially handicapped youngsters as there is in any generalizing about groups. No two children are alike. There is no way to predict reliably which child in a family of children subjected to neglect and brutality will become socially or emotionally handicapped or whether any one of them will.

There are, however, certain statements that can be made about their needs for rehabilitation. First, let us consider the factors which might be involved in the development of the socially troubled individual. For the sake of brevity, short descriptive phrases are used. Of course not all of these factors are found in any one child's history or personality.

Environmental factors: parents separated, missing, or in conflict; no parent with positive appreciation and affection for child; one parent overbearing; domination by mother; brutality, sadism, and hatreds; swearing and vulgar atmosphere; early witnessing of abusive sexual intercourse; physical neglect; many adults without one person in authority; multiracial and multireligious family; family mobility; high aspiration by parent for low-ability youngster; poor relationships among children in family; adults saying one thing and meaning something else; narcotic and alcoholic abuse; inconsistency in discipline; controls by harsh punishment and rejection; no preparation for school-learning in the environment.

Cultural factors: low-class, nonverbal group; crowded substandard urban housing; educationally barren; minority ethnic group; no life experiences beyond immediate neighborhood; lack of awareness of good cultural opportunities immediately available; "second-class" social group; low aspiration of adults; few recreational facilities; low regard for youth; few family fun experiences; nonreading adults.

Educational status: functioning below chronological age and intellectual ability; defiant; fails to appreciate long-range learning goals; quarrelsome with other students; unable to accept authority of teacher or administrators; slightly below normal intelligence; bright and bored; poor study habits; lack of cultural experiences necessary for educational readiness; needs remedial instruction; progressively deteriorating adjustment to school controls; unable to relate satisfactorily to teacher; irregular school attendance; mobility of family with many changes in schools; unable to accept remedial work; emotional blocks to learning; short attention span; sees no value in education.

Religious experiences: experience with inflexible religious codes; "snips and snatches" of a variety of religious concepts; lacks understanding of relationship of religious words and actual life; experience with cruelty and sin; asks basic questions in untheological ways; knows self as "bad"; sees hypocrisy in adults; has difficulty with authority and shows little inner control or conscience; unable to accept religious goals; unable to delay gratification of immediate desires; holds self-gratification as highest value; has little experience with love or acceptance; accepts validity of capricious "luck"; literalist; no image of "good" adult; fundamentalist experience with restrictions on fun associated with faith; no values of own with which to evaluate peer action; lack of sense of guilt or shame; guilt covered up by aggression; forgiveness not within personal experience; unable to judge right and wrong; moral lectures without example; no experience with an adult who exemplifies religious values; insulation built up against adult teaching; little hope for future; rebellion and search for independence; questioning of childhood beliefs because of peer rejection; holds values of peer rather than religious community; little apprehension of the spiritual.

Psychological problems: deep, complex fears and anxieties; severe emotional conflicts; sense of futility; distrust of other persons; self-mutilation by tatooing and cutting; inner desire for punishment; repressed sense of guilt; low self-esteem; feelings of insecurity and inferiority; easily discouraged by difficult tasks; strong hatreds; use of sex as a weapon against society; erotic relationships; hostility toward

27

adults; refusal to admit need of help; denial of dependency needs; conscience or superego not functioning adequately; fear of new things and change; need for immediate gratification of desires; emotional disturbances; neuroses, no independent moral values; strong defenses against inner change; places values in lower-class focus on trouble, toughness, slickness, smartness, excitement, fate, and autonomy.

Physical factors: facial or bodily disfigurement; distinctive physical stature; acne; female obesity; sight, hearing, or speech defect; inability to appreciate own appearance; minimal brain damage; lack of physical dexterity and coordination.

NEEDS OF THE SOCIALLY HANDICAPPED

The problems of socially handicapped children and youth are related to the negative characteristics just listed. While the needs of these youngsters are the same as those of all youngsters, the deprivation of these needs has contributed to the development of social handicaps. All youngsters have basic needs which must be fulfilled in one way or another if they are to have a chance to grow as healthy personalities able to live comfortably in society.

Fundamentally every child in the beginning of life needs to have an adult who loves and respects him and to whom he can relate as an independent growing self. If it is possible for a child to have both parents, so much the better. Each child needs an environment which sets consistent limits on behavior and in which acceptable activity is approved. Each child needs to have an adult whom he can trust, and whose positive goals he desires to imitate. Each child as he grows needs to have the opportunity to realize the potentials within himself, to have satisfying relationships with others, and to participate responsibly in his community.

There are many ways to describe the needs of children.

The authors mentioned in the Bibliography list them in different ways. The important point is that when these needs are not met, or only partially provided for, conflicts, anxieties, and hostilities may develop within the child. These feelings are often reflected in habitual antisocial behavior, and become a handicap to the youngster's social adjustment. The answer to why individual children in deprived conditions become handicapped, and why others do not is for the psychiatrist to ponder.

Because of his difficulties the socially maladjusted child develops exaggerated needs in certain areas of life. The following needs, very simply stated, are significant for the Christian educator.

Emotional needs. The handicapped child needs an adult or adults who will be generous toward him, respecting him and overlooking much unacceptable behavior. This adult needs to indicate in his relationships to the child: "I know you have problems now, but I like you. I know that after a while things may be different." The child needs an adult who will accept him and not his actions. "I like you, but I don't like what you are doing right now." He needs an adult who will listen, who can be trusted, and who will provide a model to imitate when the child is ready to grow. The child needs a great deal of time and patience for growing toward the point when he is no longer threatened by adults and is able to accept their values for himself.

Social needs. The handicapped child needs an environmental situation in which minimal limits are set on behavior and consistently enforced. The child needs satisfying personal contacts with other youngsters and adults which will provide an opportunity for positive experiences of living in a social community. The child needs time in which to begin to accept inner behavioral controls for himself. This help should be provided early in a youngster's life, as soon as possible after social difficulties are recognized. The child needs a variety of experiences in a social community through which he may learn what kind of action is appropriate.

Religious needs. As we proceed in suggesting needs, it becomes more and more evident that a socially handicapped child is a child in need of an accepting, loving adult. His immediate need is not for biblical information or moral pronouncements; it is for an adult who lives in trust and in love, who lives "in Christ." Christianity has always known that ultimately religion is personal. Ultimately it was in a person that God revealed himself. The person of Jesus Christ can have and does have meaning for the troubled youngster.

Thus it might be stated that the Christian education need of the socially handicapped youngster is for Christian adults who accept the child as he is and provide the love, the example, and the understanding necessary for growth toward a new life. Within this relationship of respect and support, the learning of the meaning of the Christian faith and its biblical backgrounds may begin to take place.

A more extensive consideration of Christian experience and growth may be found in chapter 5.

The description of the socially handicapped youngster in this chapter is primarily an introduction. Sociologists, psychologists, psychiatrists, educators, pastors, and others have spent years in working with the problems of these youngsters. Great advances have been made, and are being made currently, in the care and rehabilitation of troubled persons. Yet there is much still unknown about the causes and manifestations of delinquent behavior. The total mystery of personality and the interaction of persons with the environment which they encounter in life will never be fully known. This mystery is known only to God.

The problems of the socially troubled child are very

complex and deep-rooted. The youngster who has been placed under custody in an institution does not have simple behavior problems. A superintendent of a state institution for delinquent girls describes the youngsters under her care as "socially retarded" with very special problems.

They arrive resentful, withdrawn, depressed, aggressive, destructive, defiant, hating, feeling abandoned, hopeless, inferior, and "different." Many come from multiproblem families who have become troublesome to the community and have been weighed down by social, economic, and physical pressures. They usually have had negative experiences with authority, met with many anxieties, lost faith in themselves—if indeed it ever existed—and are truly the products of hostilities and explosive resentments which the community—and we [in the institution] find hard to live with. The needs of these youngsters (impossible to realize unless one knows them intimately) at times seem frightening and overwhelming.[1]

[1] From the July 1963 report to the Board of Directors of Long Lane School, Middletown, Connecticut, by Miss Ethel Mecum, superintendent.

4 / *The Teacher of the Socially Handicapped*

*

"I THINK a teacher should know what she's talking about," one sixteen-year-old girl said.

"I liked the way Mrs. Maramarco helped us with our own questions," a second girl added.

A third commented, "The teacher should be friendly and smile, I think."

A group of teen-age girls in Long Lane School, a state institution at Middletown, Connecticut, were expressing at random to the author their ideas about the kind of teacher they wanted for Christian education classes. One girl mentioned a teacher whom they had especially liked. After the teacher's death the class wrote a tribute to her with the help of another teacher. They stated that they knew teaching them was part of her job, but they were glad their group was one she taught. The following are portions of the tribute which seem to go beyond the expected polite phrases to express something of their relationship with Phyllis Maramarco and their appreciation of her as a person:

> We remember Mrs. Maramarco as the kind of person who was: happy and smiling, . . . honest, . . . cheerful even when she was in pain. She cheered us up when we arrived in class feeling mad at the world.
>
> She helped us be better Christians and disciples of Jesus Christ: by making God seem more personal, . . . by really

believing and living what she taught. We are so thankful that she could be our teacher. We will always remember her because she has become a part of us.

Two characteristics of a teacher seem to sum up the feelings of the girls. That person must be someone (1) who listens to what they are asking and (2) who knows what he is talking about both through experience and study.

At first the request that a teacher "listen to what they are asking" seems easy to fulfill. All one needs are some ears, and maybe a smile. It is not as easy as that. Involved is the ability of the teacher to create an environment in which the aggressive, troubled youngster can speak. It is not easy to break down lifelong defenses built up to protect inner feelings. It is not easy to help these youngsters feel free to ask questions related to something they really care about. To ask such questions means to them the possibility of further hurt or ridicule. Often they cannot even deal with their basic questions, nor can they put them into words.

In order to create an environment in which feelings may be dealt with, the teacher must be a stable, mature person, who lives the Christian life he teaches. He must know himself and be realistic about his own needs and limitations. As a part of the institutional team of adults, the Christian teacher may be one of the first adults about whom the socially handicapped youngster has ever come to care. In participating in cottage life in some institutions, the teacher will be part of a total atmosphere created by the staff and previous teachers which encourages trust and response on the part of the students. The teacher will need to "be himself" in this environment and become known as a person with particular interests, talents, and concerns, a person who respects other persons.

As youngsters begin to grow to trust an adult, they begin to accept, to imitate, and to develop a bit in self-esteem. They may want to be like this person who likes them and cares about them. Thus the teacher over a long period of time may create an atmosphere of acceptance where children and youth feel secure enough to begin to deal with the basic values of life. Further discussion of the need of acceptance of children and youth is in chapter 5.

Once while sitting in church next to a teen-age girl who was in custody of an institution, the author noted the girl subtly watching her. Slowly the girl began to tug at her skirt which was well above her knees. She studied her tattooed arms, rubbing them a bit. She stared at her nails now chewed down the side of her fingers. For a moment these things seemed to be important to her. She wanted to be like a person she admired for the moment.

General Characteristics of the Teacher

Here are some of the important attitudes and abilities mentioned repeatedly by chaplains, educators, and psychologists as important assets of a person who is effective as a teacher in the world of the socially handicapped youngster. These characteristics represent an ideal person who does not exist; however, a good teacher tends to be the kind of person:

» who is finding fulfillment in his own personal life
» who likes other persons
» who can like a youngster regardless of his past or present acting out of rebellion
» who can accept aggressive behavior, knowing that it is part of a youngster's way of reacting to the hostile world he has known
» who does not need to have every youngster like him
» who does not feel underneath that the youngster must be punished for the past
» who does not find gratification of his own conflicts and sexual frustrations in the sordid lives of the youngsters

- » who can listen to youngsters and help them search for ways of expressing their real feelings
- » who does not type or prejudge persons and sees only those actions which fit the type
- » who can accept different social class levels without pity or judgment
- » who can enjoy all children regardless of physical appearance
- » who can accept and appreciate self-goals of youngsters which do not include the hope of a college education
- » who can accept youngsters' religious experiences as important and meaningful to them, even when they differ from the teacher's experience
- » who can trust youngsters' abilities to think and make decisions for themselves
- » who can accept youngsters as a product of their past experiences, and knows that they can change and grow in their own way
- » who knows each individual in the group
- » who accepts and loves the youngster regardless of unpleasant disruptive behavior
- » who is able to be critical of self and profit from errors in judgment in the teaching situation
- » who has the ability to enforce rules once established in the class
- » who trusts God's grace and his creative power in each new moment of time.

This list of characteristics of a superior teacher of socially handicapped youngsters may seem to be overwhelming. It is, but its requirements are not more than those of a superior teacher in any teaching situation. It might be noted that there is no mention of age, race, sex, formal education, economic status, or professional training in therapy. However one plea must be made in this area. Male teachers are especially needed. If one parent has been missing from a troubled youngster's life, it is most often the father. Youngsters in custodial care need to have opportunities to be with men who hold Christian values and who care enough about them to give them their time.

SPECIAL CONSIDERATIONS FOR THE TEACHER

There are several areas of the teacher's relationship with the students and the institution which seem to need special emphasis because of the particular circumstances of the total teaching situation.

Social class and cultural gaps. The United States is a land of diverse people. We brag about this. Some sociologists claim that persons may change their social and economic status so readily that there actually exists no real class structure; however, there is a major group of persons "in the middle" to whom the term middle class is applied. It is from this middle social and economic group that the teacher of exceptional children generally comes. This middle group, as other groups, does have a set of values and styles of living which are characteristic. The style of thinking and acting of this group often permeates a person to the extent that other ways of living appear to be of less value. Much of current advertising is geared to this group as well as school education. The person in the middle group tends to like to accumulate "'nice" things, values academic education, wants to "get ahead" in life, has some interest in creative expression, and values the family in ideal if not in fact. The middle group predominates in the "established" churches and influences church programming and the terms in which the gospel is expressed.

Between the middle group and other groups there is often very little communication or appreciation. There is a social gap between lives which is not normally bridged without effort. Persons in the middle group tend to fail to appreciate differing social patterns of living. They often fail to appreciate the warmth, friendliness, and shared concern of the crowded urban apartment house, honesty about basic physical aspects of life, activities which are more physical than intellectual, lives based on expressed desires for excitement and motion, the support and "belongingness" found in small subgroups of society within the more impersonal city, and satisfaction in physical work as an occupation.

There are cultural gaps also. English-speaking persons tend to fail to appreciate the intelligence, values, and styles of living of the non-English-speaking world, except as tourist attractions.

Within the urban institution social, economic, and cultural groups are mixed. The gaps must be bridged if communication and effective teaching are to take place. At first bridging the gaps is primarily the responsibility of the teacher, in whatever way these gaps are manifested.

Facility with Christian concepts. Referring back to the initial conversation of this chapter, we note that one of the things which the girls stated they appreciated in a teacher was knowledge about what the group was discussing. A teacher himself should be continually learning so that he is able to express Christian concepts in many new and fresh ways, relevant to the lives of children and youth. Such a teacher is able to listen to youngsters' expression of feeling and experience, let them deal with basic questions, such as, "Who is God, anyway?" and then be able to gather together the ideas expressed in a manner which is consistent with Christian faith and in terms of the youngsters' experiences. A good teacher is continually growing in his faith. An example of the use of facility with theology in discussion is found on pages 82-83.

Cooperative teaching. The Christian educator in teaching persons in custody is, in many respects, part of the institutional team. Also, as a classroom teacher, he may be one of several persons working with the same group of children. Many persons with whom the teacher works will have greater experience and understanding in specialized fields. This fact sometimes leads to conflicts. Further, among adults working together there is the possibility of friction between personalities. The teacher needs to be aware that his relationships with other adults are discernable by youngsters in the institutional community and his Christian witness is evaluated in terms of these relationships. Chapter 8 considers the relationship of the Christian educator with the institution.

Living with youngsters. A teacher is a person too. Each teacher has a particular talent, interest, and style of teaching. The genuineness of a person being himself and using his special talents is appreciated by all youngsters. Mrs. Maramarco, mentioned early in the chapter, and her husband, shared their musical talents with many classes. A teacher with talent in art might use this medium to help youngsters express on paper, or in other materials, their inner feelings. Living with youngsters means sharing oneself, not the details of daily life, but the interests and the enthusiasms which make a person unique and special. This kind of specialness helps a youngster to find his specialness too.

Growing with youngsters. The teacher grows too! How many times teachers have said, "I learned more than the children did!" Not only is there new insight gained by the teacher in the subject matter, but with patience and respect, something is learned from the pupils too. Together teacher and student deal with the issues of faith on the level where things matter, fiercely and emotionally sometimes.

Most good teachers feel that each teaching experience is new and unique, requiring critical evaluation of past teaching and sharp thinking about the present situation. With this attitude the teacher grows as he provides opportunities for the students to grow.

The teacher is the most important part of the Christian education program for socially troubled children and youth. He may teach with minimum space and materials, but if he is a mature adult who accepts unlovely youngsters and believes in the possibility of their Christian growth, the physical environment is secondary. The latest and best materials and curriculum guides are of little worth if the person working with these youngsters does not in himself exemplify the Christian truth about which he speaks.

The teacher ultimately must be the support and the example which make possible inner struggle and searching on the part of troubled youngsters and which furnish direction in which to grow.

5 / Influences for Christian Growth

MEET JUDY

"Judy, an attractive girl of fifteen, lived with her mother and father in an intact home. Her two sisters and brother, ages 16, 14, and 18 respectively, live in an average neighborhood adjoining a deteriorating area. During the past two years all of the children have become involved in antisocial behavior. The mother is a member of the Pentecostal Church and is unusually strict with the children. The children have been required to accompany the mother to church every night except Saturday. They are not allowed any recreation or association with other teen-agers. Jewelry, lipstick, and dancing are not permitted. As Judy and her siblings have grown into adolescence, they have become increasingly rebellious and hostile. Judy, an extremely attractive girl, has become sullen and defiant, refuses to go to school regularly, has begun to fraternize with undesirables and has given vent to her hostility by setting two fires, one in a wastebasket, and another to an American flag at school. When she finally began to abscond from home over a period of months, she was brought before the court and committed to a training school. The resident social worker is working with Judy while the field social worker of the institution is trying to help the parents develop insight into the needs and problems which their children present."[1]

---

[1] A case reported by Chaplain Harold G. Nixon.

In contrast to many delinquent youngsters Judy comes to an institution with extensive religious experience and knowledge. Yet Judy presents to the Christian educator many of the same problems as youngsters who have no experience in the church. Judy has religious knowledge, but she also has very negative feelings about religion. The Christian faith has no positive meaning for her life. Judy, in spite of her intellectual knowledge is a sinner—in the language of the Christian.

THEOLOGICAL FOUNDATIONS FOR CHRISTIAN GROWTH

Jesus said: "I came not to call the righteous, but sinners" (Mark 2:17).

"Sinner" is a label which we tend to assign to persons who cause trouble in the community. "Sin" is an ancient word. It was part of Jesus' vocabulary. It describes self-centered acts and thoughts which hurt the self and others. Sin involves putting one's self, or something else, at the center of life instead of God. In sin self-interest becomes the basis of action instead of the love of God as known in Jesus Christ. The sin most quickly condemned by people is the sin manifest in antisocial behavior.

On this basis socially handicapped youngsters are judged sinners, since they do not conform to the behavior expected of "nice" persons who stay out of trouble. Surely these youngsters do steal, commit sex offenses, and are often disobedient to parents and teachers. In truth, they are sinners. But so are all persons, even those who refrain from lawbreaking, even those who belong to the church and try to live Christian lives. Sin is more than wrong action, it is putting the self or something else instead of God in the center of one's inner life. No person is without sin, for no one lives solely for God. The delinquent person and other persons are not two different kinds of beings. All are sinners, each in his own way. Even a Christian such as Paul

41

wrote: "For I do not do the good I want, but the evil I do not want is what I do" (Rom. 7:19). Jesus said, "No one is good but God alone" (Luke 18:19).

Jesus knew people. He saw their sin and he helped them. To the paralytic he said, "Your sins are forgiven," and the paralytic by faith walked (Luke 5:20, 25). Jesus listened to the questioning of the rich young ruler, recognized the source of his separation from God, and said, "One thing you still lack" (Luke 18:22). When John the Baptist first saw Jesus he said, "Behold, the Lamb of God, who takes away the sin of the world!" (John 1:29) Jesus came to help sinners. His teachings are not rules to punish people or to take the joy out of life, but to free them to be new persons.

It is the faith of Christians that Jesus' death atoned for man's persistent sin. Because of Christ, man need not bear the cumulative weight of his daily sin. Paul, the redeemed in Christ, crys out: "Wretched man that I am! Who will deliver me from this body of death? Thanks be to God through Jesus Christ our Lord!" (Rom. 7:24-25) Through God's free gift of forgiveness and love in Christ, man is saved from the fate of his sin, if man so chooses.

CHRIST'S FORGIVENESS AND HEALING TODAY

Today God in Jesus Christ still forgives the sin of the world and heals the sickness of sinners. By the presence of his living Spirit we may be made new persons. It is God in his own way who brings about the healing and change. True, for most this healing comes through the help of persons who have discovered how to use the powers for strength and growth existing within man, God's creature. It is this inner capacity of movement toward wholeness, toward physical and spiritual health, with which the psychiatrist, the therapist, the social worker, the counselor, the pastor, and the educator, work. The religious worker, physician, or scientist believes that God heals through the skill and the knowledge of men and women who care for those in need.

The Christian educator, using the knowledge of science about man, works with God to lead persons toward new lives in Christ. School educators and psychologists constantly contribute to the fund of knowledge about the ways persons learn and the ways in which they can be best stimulated to learn. This knowledge cannot be ignored by the Christian because it is being discovered outside of the church. The discoverer of truth is unimportant. If this truth is found to be in harmony with God's revealed truth in Jesus Christ and will serve to increase the teaching competence of the Christian educator, he cannot afford to ignore it. God works in many ways among men to accomplish his purposes.

Not all sickness, either physical or mental, is the result of sin. Jesus affirmed this. The child with measles, the woman with cancer, or the man born blind about whom Jesus spoke in John 9:3 do not suffer necessarily because they have sinned. Not all physical or mental illness can be blamed on sin, although physicians are currently emphasizing the importance of the influence of the emotions and mind upon the body. Man is a creature created by God with a physical body which is subject to disease and death. To be a creature is not a sin. Man's sin lies in the way he uses his life, as a creature, for himself. His sin is the way in which he tries to act—as the creator, as infallible, all-knowing, and of more importance than anyone else.

Not all antisocial behavior is sin. Someone has to stand up and denounce accepted injustice. The society in which man lives is not perfect. Injustices do exist in our customs, in our laws, and in our classrooms. Too often judgments of right and wrong by society rest on questionable bias or tradition. Society tends to preserve what is, rather than to change what is wrong. People tend to avoid critical evaluation of old, accepted practices and routines. Outdated customs cause trouble for some, especially teen-agers who are anxious to try new ways. All youngsters who break the laws of society do not deserve to be labeled as depraved sinners because they have rebelled against intolerable pressures within their home, or against the prejudices and sin of society as a whole as it has ignored the needs of the youngsters. Although the delinquents' action may be more violent and their behavior more unpleasant, they share in the sin of all. It is not unforgivable. It is not completely hopeless.

INFLUENCES FOR CHRISTIAN GROWTH

There are a number of Christian affirmations related to the growth of persons as Christians. The order of these affirmations and the vocabulary are arbitrary; their sum is the hope of the educator who is committed to leading troubled youngsters toward new lives through Christ.

All persons are creatures of God. Being human is not a sin. Life, sickness, and death are part of being a creature. Sin lies in denying the self as a creature created by God. Sin, anxiety, conflict, and confusion result from thinking of oneself as God instead of as creature dependent upon the Creator. It lies in denying God, as revealed in Jesus Christ, as the center of life and all meaning.

Freedom is the gift of all. In spite of early environmental pressures and hurts, in spite of circumstances and conditions into which a person is born, a person is yet free with God's help (and man's) to choose the kind of person he will be and to change.

God is present with men. God has revealed himself to men in his world and in Jesus Christ. His power and his love are present with men, guiding and helping those who

44

allow him to do so. Man has available to him a knowledge of God's will for him through the Bible and through prayer.

This is God's world. Those who accept God's rule live in harmony with the essence of God's continuing creation. Being on "the Lord's side" is living with forces of creative growth and redemption. God's creative power acts against the negative, hurtful forces which many troubled children have known. God is for them and for health.

God judges his people. God does expect love, devotion, reverence, obedience of his people. There are discernible values by which man must live if he would do God's will. God's will and his way for man are made known in the Bible and to man in our time by God's Spirit. It is through God's judgment that we recognize our sin and may repent.

God forgives and redeems. God does not desire that man should succumb to evil. God offers help, accepts the requests of man for forgiveness, and gives support to the new person groping toward acceptance of his love. It is the faith of Christians that God ultimately triumphs over sin and evil, that he is participating in the life of man. This is the resurrection faith. In spite of all that man could do to Christ, God was ultimately victorious on Easter morning.

God works through persons. God chose to reveal himself in a person—Jesus of Nazareth. God's love, forgiveness, and redemption are most meaningfully expressed today in the love, respect, care, acceptance, witness, and self-sacrifice of persons. Men have a responsibility to extend to others the love and support necessary for their well-being and fulfillment as persons.

God heals and works miracles. God's power is ultimate and his ways are not completely knowable to man whom he created. Unpredictable healings take place even today; forces are at work which are not entirely accountable by the laws which man has discovered. God lives in his world and no person need be without hope even when under seemingly intolerable pressures and conditions.

Needs for Christian Growth[2]

If we are to meet the needs of the institutionalized youngster, we must be deeply aware of the emotional and spiritual deprivations which the child has known. In a sense the institutionalized youngster has distinctive needs even though basically they are the needs of all children. It is only as certain very elemental spiritual needs are met that these youngsters may be lead into a more meaningful and wholesome relationship with their Creator. An understanding of these needs lies at the base of planning Christian education programs. The following needs are listed in a reasonably logical and natural sequence.

The need to experience acceptance. Many institutionalized youngsters have experienced a lifetime of rejection and cruelty. Many of them were not wanted even before conception as well as during pregnancy and after birth. Because of wide and agonizing rejection by parents, followed by estrangements from the school, the community, and the church, these youngsters have a low self-esteem. They feel small, inadequate, weak, fearful, and unworthy, and perceive a pervasive emptiness. Out of these feelings there grows a need to fail and to destroy oneself because one cannot succeed. A number of boys have an undue fascination with death, and particularly the electric chair or gas chamber.

Since most institutionalized youngsters have been disappointed in general by adults who have either rejected them or not cared about them, it is understandable that they will often seek their identity from their own kind.

[2] The remainder of this chapter is condensed from a paper by Chaplain John C. Gould.

Herein lies the appeal of the gangs. Even though it be in fantasy, the titles "The Knights," "The Dukes," and even "The Chaplains," give them a sense of identity and importance.

These youngsters in their relationships with adults in the institution require relationships of genuine acceptance. Such an acceptance will go a long way toward overcoming the general pervasive estrangement which they have known, although it can never replace the initial family love which was lost.

Acceptance is an experience and not an intellectual concept. If youngsters are to know that they are accepted by God, they must know something of the meaning of the word by experience.

The need for dependence. Every person needs things, but more particularly, they need persons upon whom they can lean and depend. The normal child learns to depend on God because he is surrounded by parents and family on whom he can naturally depend. Institutionalized youngsters often have not found this degree of sustenance and support. Our agencies are a poor substitute for this, but apparently substitute we must.

This need for dependence often is covered up by strong denials or disguised in acts of stealing or an attitude of pseudoindependence. Because these youngsters have not been able to depend on anyone, they frequently feel the necessity to manipulate adults for their own ends; and often from their prayers and attitudes toward religious figures one gains the feeling that they have a need to magically manipulate God. Yet underneath it all, they are so terribly and desperately dependent.

The need for a framework of reference. In a logical sequence, if youngsters have found acceptance and have found people they can depend upon, they can become available to searching for an intelligent framework within which they can build their lives and begin to bring some order out of disorder.

At first institutionalized youngsters may seem to say, "Don't fence me in," but in fact, they are saying, "Please give me the skeletal framework to withstand the disintegrating pressures and forces which threaten my destruction." One can almost see a child moving from being an unstructured blob of protoplasm to being a person. It is at this stage that law and order of things can begin to become intelligible rather than instruments of further deprivation.

This has implications in regard to discipline. Institutionalized boys frequently ask and want to know: "Is this right?" or "Is this wrong?" In so doing, they seem to be asking for a framework and if this need is not met in their developmental years, they may be incapable of appropriately using freedom later on.

A framework of reference involves a set of values by which one can evaluate experiences and make decisions for day-by-day living. A religious orientation provides such a set of values.

The need for acceptance of selfhood. It seems to be generally characteristic that institutionalized youngsters do not have any strong sense of identity, that is, they are not able to answer the basic question "Who am I and what is my purpose in life?" They tend to borrow their identity from their immediate environment with considerable vacillation and confusion. Their parents tend to add to their confusion either by not being available or by rejecting them. Therefore they may look about them for a strong person, but such persons are usually strong from the viewpoint of the jungle rather than that of humanity. They are also easily influenced by their peers in spite of their conflicts with them.

It is only after they find acceptance and are able to depend upon individuals whom they can count on that they begin to have a sense of self-worth. It is then that they can see value in themselves as children of God, particularly as they are able to try new experiences and find new undiscovered talents within themselves.

In the institutional setting, however, there must be a continual awareness of the real relationship between staff and children. It is easy for adults as human beings to slip into functioning mechanically and routinely, going through the motions of caring without having the feeling behind it. It is then natural for the children to react with the feeling that we do not really care for them, that we are only doing this because we are being paid for it. When this happens, of course, the relationship is lost. It is difficult for the relationship to be established in the first place because these children have been hurt so often that they are naturally suspicious and distrustful. This is particularly true of children of minority groups, having faced social rejection as well as rejection within the family.

The need for acceptance of responsibility. This comes with the acceptance of self. Many youngsters feel the compulsion to lie and to present a facade of other than what they are. This would seem to spring from their low self-esteem and lack of self-identity. Frequently they fall back on a magical concept and fantasy; for instance, one boy felt the necessity to talk at great length about the heroic accomplishments of his father in his military career. Actually he had known desertion by his father, whose military career was anything but heroic. Jimmie hung on to these fantasies, however, for a long time until he found a new identity in his relationships at the institution. As he began to emerge as a real person in his own right, the fantasies lessened and disappeared.

Learning to accept responsibility means also the acceptance of the guilt of failure without projecting the blame on someone else. It is important that youth realize that they are not damned or predestined to failure, but rather that to err is human. Part of a healthy sense of guilt is not accepting unrealistic guilt such as being responsible for the separation of one's parents. As institutionalized youth are able to see in proper perspective the finitude and the failures of man as well as his nobility and virtues, they can become more realistic in their human relationships. Often they can begin to accept their parents as they are without totally rejecting them or obliterating the perception of their faults by fantasy.

The need to utilize external spiritual resources. Youngsters seem to be able to make only limited use of the resources of religion until the above prior needs have been at least partially fulfilled. In the disorganized existences which they have previously known it may be that they have been exposed to the church, but have found only primitive ideas of God and of being a Christian. It is significant, too, that they usually conceive of God as being remote and distant rather than as the eternal, abiding, all-pervading Spirit.

It is also as they develop as human beings that they can see that the church is more than a building where people perform a duty or obligation. They are able to see that it is a broad fellowship and not simply a group of persons who pray and read the Bible. It is of critical importance that youngsters become aware that there is a real and meaningful relationship between religion and life experiences.

There is a danger that we fall short of our greater responsibility by emphasizing only a person's ability to make a satisfactory adjustment in work, in school, and in other areas.

The need to care for others. The capacity to give of oneself comes last in our order of sequence of need. It is as other needs are met that one is able to contribute to the needs of other people. The staff in a sensitive program of care will be giving a great deal of themselves to the youngsters. It is a mistake, however, to allow this to be all a one-way street. Our youth need to have the opportunities to make a contribution to others by way of working for others —by gifts and by making significant contributions through their talents. The responsibility for pets is another avenue of giving. If "It is better to give than to receive" is to be more than a cliché, then institutionalized youth need to be able to give and to experience not only being cared for, but caring.

6 / Curriculum Decisions

*

A NUMBER of important curriculum decisions must be made in planning Christian education for socially handicapped children and youth. In all these decisions the nature of the children and the nature of the Christian faith are central. The goal of the Christian education program is to guide youngsters with special needs in a search for new meaning for their lives in the Christian experience. Or as one experienced worker with youth states the goal: "It is to discover what the problems, needs, and possibilities of the child are and then to relate the Christian gospel to those needs. The gospel is relevant to the question of finding out where the child is and then helping him relate that to his faith."[1]

The socially handicapped youngster brings to the religious education class certain special characteristics, as described in chapter 3. The Christian faith is relevant to their problems. Jesus' ministry was to the lost as well as to the religiously comfortable person; in fact, it was the sinner about whom he was most concerned.

The Christian educator working with children having special needs and handicaps is involved in curriculum decision-making in a way not characteristic of the regular Sunday church school teacher. Teachers of socially handicapped

---

[1] From correspondence with Robert Scott, Youth Division, Department of Corrections, State of Michigan.

children must make many curriculum decisions which are normally made for them in the standard Sunday church school material. There is little curriculum specifically prepared for these troubled youngsters whose backgrounds differ considerably from those of the middle-class church family. In the institutional setting there is no superintendent of special instruction to help decide the kind of program best suited to the needs of specific classes. In fact the administrator of the institution may himself look to the religious educator for direction and suggestions. As it was pointed out in chapter 4, a superior teacher is required for traveling the untraveled roads toward Christian education for the socially handicapped.

ADMINISTRATIVE DECISIONS

There are certain decisions which must be made which are mainly administrative. These decisions involve such matters as size of classes, length of session, grouping, and session structure.

Size of classes. It is essential to have small classes for socially handicapped youngsters. Eight to ten children would be an ideal number. There are several reasons for the need of small groups. The youngsters are individuals with very different backgrounds and needs. A teacher cannot relate himself successfully to the individual and be sensitive to individual problems and questions if the group is large. The kind of growth in Christian faith these youngsters need is dependent upon a small group situation. Attitudes of trust and respect grow out of close relationships with a person who exemplifies these attitudes. The youngsters need to feel they belong, in a sense, to the adult before they emulate him.

Youngsters who have been starved by lack of approval and affection are hungry for important person-to-person relationships with accepting adults. These youngsters can become quite demanding of attention once they find an adult who seems to care. Their need in religious education is not the drill of information or the lecture, characteristic of the large-group situation, but the personal experience of Christian living which comes from being cared about personally by an adult who is available and responsive to immediate questions and demands.

If the group is too large, the aggression and defiance, typical of rebellious children, might become overwhelming.

Length of session. The session should allow time for a variety of activities and creative experiences, such as writing prayers and participation in short-term service projects. It should allow for deep exploration of questions and ideas, if the group is old enough and has reached this point in its relationships. The time should be short enough so that the group will not be bored and turn to socially unacceptable behavior.

A period of forty-five minutes to an hour would allow for a combination of serious study, informal conversation, some physical participation such as map-making, and possibly singing. In a twenty- or thirty-minute period two different focuses of attention might be included, with variety from session to session. Regardless of the time allotment, however, the period should not be used entirely by the teacher himself for lecture or presentation of materials.

In the institutional setting the time schedule will probably depend on the overall program. Time for the class may be assigned on a regular basis. Flexibility is desirable so that important experiences are not cut in the middle.

Grouping of youngsters. Grouping is very important because it helps the pupil and teacher work more effectively together; however, there are no one-two-three rules which can be applied to grouping of children and youth in any situation. Groups may be formed according to age, mental ability, interest in physical activities such as crafts, interest in discussing religious ideas, or some other factors. There is no one "best" way to group any more than there is any one "superior" way of learning. The most effective grouping moves toward putting together children who learn in similar ways and who are at particular stages of their physical and mental development. Such grouping allows for a more appropriate choice of curriculum and materials. Often grouping in a religious educational program needs to be adjusted as pupils and teachers become better acquainted. Grouping is a tool which educators use to make possible more effective teaching; it should not become so fixed and traditional that it interferes with the total purpose of the program. Also it should be noted that groups ought not to be made so homogeneous that individuals lose the stimulation for learning provided by the interaction of differences.

Session structure. Completeness in each session is important. The population in institutions is constantly changing. The aim of many institutions is to rehabilitate youngsters and return them to the community as soon as it seems advisable and possible. Also, attendance at class may be interrupted by other factors in the life of the institution. It should be noted here that when attendance has been irregular, personal contacts must be made with individual youngsters to assure them that they are wanted and liked.

When each session seems complete, a feeling of satisfaction and accomplishment is enjoyed. These are two feelings often missing in the lives of socially troubled youngsters. Yet some group plan or suggestion for the sessions to come will tend to be encouraging to the class. The teacher's enthusiastic presentation of long-term goals may be of positive value for youngsters who tend to find life important only at the moment they live it. The ability to deny immediate, less desirable experiences in favor of greater, long-term values is not only a characteristic of the mature person, it is a characteristic view of the Christian.

Decisions on curriculum content should be based upon the needs and interests of the youngsters of a particular group, keeping in mind the eventual necessity of developing a basic understanding of the Bible and the meaning of the Christian faith for life. Neither the child nor the content of the faith should be the exclusive determining factor. A lecture to teen-agers on the Gospel of John might have a place in the total Christian education program of a local church, but for these youngsters it would probably be an entire waste of time. It may even drive them away from future sessions and confirm their suspicions about the irrelevant nature of Christianity. The whims of the youngsters should not entirely determine the content either. Aimless, wandering conversations will not satisfy the real inner need of these youngsters for understanding the basic nature of their lives and for establishing goals and values for themselves. They do want to learn even at the time they protest the most, providing the teacher can arrange a point where their interests and the content of the faith meet.

Two basic approaches to curriculum content are suggested here. Both are valuable. Briefly they are: (1) an approach through youngsters' personal questions about religion, and (2) an approach through studies of specific areas of content of the faith. Neither of these approaches is the right way for all groups, nor should either be used exclusively with any group. In fact, to separate the two does violence to the teaching program as a whole. Persons and the faith cannot be separated if teaching is to be meaningful; however, some educators prefer to begin with emphasis on one aspect rather than the other.

Approach through youngsters' questions. Many experienced chaplains and teachers prefer to begin work with youngsters in an informal manner which encourages students to ask questions about religious matters of concern to them. Here are some questions that one group of institutionalized girls asked to discuss with a religious counselor whom they knew and trusted:

» Why do some people feel better than others?
» Why aren't we trusted?
» How can one be certain one has the right religion?
» How can we regain faith? And keep it?
» How do we feel Christ inside?
» Why does God have so many names?
» How do we get close to God?
» Why isn't prayer answered?
» Why do we go to church?

These serious questions are asked by persons who have experienced hatred, loneliness, and despair perhaps unknown to the secure middle-class teacher. Superficial answers, by an adult who is sure he has all the answers, would be a violation of the trust the girls felt in venturing to ask the questions. A child who has got into trouble with the courts for acting out rebellion and frustration growing out of situations which she is entirely incapable of changing really does not understand why she has been institutionalized, or why she is not trusted. Girls who have been institutionalized for repeated sex offenses may feel that they were just doing something to give them status in their group. They may have sought, as adolescents, to imitate the satisfaction which they observed adults to find in sex. It was one way to grow up fast! Somehow these acts are approved and bragged about among peers, and practiced among adults, but are unacceptable to the juvenile court authorities. Why isn't a girl trusted? She may have been arrested simply because she was caught doing what others do. What has God got to do with all of this?

These real questions may become the basis of a number

of short discussion or study units, or one question may be considered each week. There are advantages for the student and the teacher in planning at least one week ahead. The student may do some thinking and anticipating, and the teacher must do some preparation. Teacher preparation, however, does not mean preparation of a lecture. It should mean an investigation of the general area of Bible or theology involved in the question. This means reading, thinking, and talking with others—including the institution's staff —about the subject and about the meaning it might have for the group. Those responsible for the counseling of students in the institution will have very helpful suggestions to make. Under the teacher's guidance, the group may push and pull at the question until hidden fears and thoughts, usually considered unacceptable to persons in authority, are expressed and evaluated. This does not mean, of course, that final answers are arrived at or that thinking about the subject ends with that session.

There are a number of *cautions* which must be mentioned here. First is the caution raised by the experienced youth worker. It is pointed out that youngsters may easily take advantage of a teacher who accepts too readily superficial questions aimed at engaging the group in a kind of fencing game. Many keen delinquents are experts in repartee with sincere, well-meaning adults. Their conversations may be filled with religious clichés which have absolutely no meaning for the youngster.

Second, in a discussion of questions asked by the youngsters, the teacher should be careful to deal with experiences and words which have meaning for everyday life. A word such as immortality might be replaced by phrases such as "life after death." Involved in the term immortality are the questions: "What difference does it make how you live now?" "What happens to your body?" "Do you ever see God?" The traditional Christian vocabulary may be familiar to the youngsters due to slang usage, but the Christian meanings are distant from their experience. Such terms as "God, the Father," "infinite," "sin," "saved," and others are all suspect until their meanings have been carefully worked out with the youngsters.

Third, the teacher should not allow the discussion to degenerate into a listing of complaints about the institution or the church. It is important for the teacher in an institution to establish his purpose as helping youngsters to think about religious questions. He is not an employee of the institution (except perhaps in the case of a chaplain) and has nothing to say about staff or administrative policies except positive encouragement. Such questions as "What do you think of my cottage parents?" or "Why doesn't the cottage doctor look at my throat?" may be acknowledged or directed to the proper authority. Cottage life is not within the realm of the teacher's responsibility. It may be expected that at one time or another youngsters will try to use the teacher as a weapon against the authority of the institution. (See chapter 8 for a discussion of the teacher's relationship to the institution.)

Fourth, basing curriculum content upon youngsters' questions requires that the teacher have considerable facility with Bible and theology. This means that the teacher is able to move from one idea to another with accuracy and fundamental knowledge of the underlying theological concepts involved. It means that the teacher is able to keep the discussion from becoming what is known as "religion in general." Thus the group will not be dealing with general subjects such as "being good," or "loving your neighbor," without considering the basic biblical teachings involved and their demands upon living.

Fifth, an educational program which releases troubled youngsters to discuss and examine their fundamental values in life should be closely related to the institutional program of psychotherapy. While the Christian educator may not be considered part of the professional team of counselors, social workers, and therapists, he will not usually find his work contrary to their basic philosophy and treatment procedures, nor irrelevant to their work. Cooperation with the treatment team is highly desirable and training from them would be most profitable. While the primary aim of the institution is not Christian growth for persons, their hopes for youngsters are not contrary to the hopes of Christian educators, nor is scientific knowledge about the way persons grow and change out of harmony with Christian belief. Truth is truth, no matter who discovers it. (There is more about this in chapter 5.) Specific suggestions for discussions are made in chapter 7.

Approach through content areas. Church school teachers often feel more at home with a teaching program which begins from an outline of specific religious content and objectives. After considerable study of the general problems and backgrounds of socially troubled youngsters, it might be decided that a unit of study based on Jesus' relationship with persons in the New Testament might be helpful. Through such a unit the youngsters might see Jesus' love and respect of persons in operation and then, or concurrently, begin to understand the meaning of love and respect in their own lives. The content of the unit would offer objective material for discussion which would not initially demand that the youngsters reveal personal feelings which at the moment they are unable to handle.

The teacher, with the group, might decide upon things they would like to study. The choice of content will depend upon the age of the youngsters and their interests. Younger children might study portions of Jesus' life or the structure of the Bible. Older adolescents might choose Jesus' parables or church history (with emphasis on major events of world significance). One group might study Jesus' life in relation to the church year—Christmas, Good Friday, Easter, and Pentecost.

One chaplain describes a session on the study of Joseph and his brothers. In this description one observes how the teacher leads the group from the biblical study to present-life meanings.

They saw the story on a filmstrip and then began to discuss it. They talked about the brothers and what a bad deal Joseph got. Finally one of the boys asked if God knew that they were going to do wrong when they did it. Melvin said that God knew it was going to happen and wanted Joseph to get thrown into the pit. "No," came the chorus from the group. Then the discussion became very intense. Does God know that you are going to rob a bank? Does God want us here at [the institution]? Does God know when we are about to commit suicide? All of these ideas came from the group as a result of one story. They struggled with their own questions until they seemed to be unable to go further. I felt that it was then time to give my own interpretation. In essence I illustrated my answer by using two objects which were on the table at the time; one stood for "right" and the other stood for "wrong." As I moved my finger between "right" and "wrong" I explained that at this point the choice becomes ours to make. God does not choose for us, but he does know our past choices. If we have been making wrong decisions or choices, God can expect us to continue to make such choices unless we want to change. One way prayer helps us, I continued, is that it strengthens our ability to change when we have been making wrong decisions.[2]

Certain *cautions* regarding the content approach should be noted. First, the teacher's familiarity with the content approach is a major obstacle to the use of this approach with troubled youngsters in an institution. The situation and the needs of the youngsters are entirely different from the local church. Numerous times in this manual it has been

---

[2] William J. Smith (chaplain, Parsons State Hospital and Training Center, Parsons, Kansas), *Religious Education: Some Observations from a Treatment Center for Adolescent Delinquents*. The Menninger Foundation, Department of Education (Reprint No. 163).

pointed out that the religious backgrounds and the ways in which these youngsters learn are very special. The teacher must be extremely critical of his usual methods of dealing with content in adapting them to the delinquent child in the institution.

Second, learning content is not the objective of the religious education program for delinquent youngsters, important as content is to a historical faith. It is the experience of religious educators who work with these youngsters that a child may have completely memorized a biblical story or scripture passage without having even a vague idea of its meaning for his life.

Third, content-centered teaching must be flexible. Often a teacher who begins a class session with particular learning objectives in mind, pursues these objectives at the expense of spontaneous and creative interests and questions expressed by the group.

Fourth, the teacher must continually evaluate the language in which traditionally the church has dealt with content. It should not be assumed that youngsters know the meaning of the words "pharisee," "love," or "God" or that they know where Palestine is located. The word love is particularly difficult because of its usage on television and in secular conversations. The use of the word may present a completely distorted idea of Christian relationships.

CHOICE OF MATERIALS

There is very little printed curriculum material which is suitable for the Christian education program for socially handicapped youngsters. Adaptation of materials is essential.

Denominational materials are heavily slanted toward the experiences of middle-class youngsters who are familiar with the language of the church. There is a strong emphasis on family groups. There tend to be stereotyped behaviors against which the delinquent youngster has already re-belled. The concept of God as Father is emphasized and it is assumed that the student knows a benevolent father in his home. The illustrations often are of middle-class life—good care, traveling to grandmother's house in the country, and so on. Such symbols of settled family life and social status are not relevant to the troubled youngster in the institution regardless of the economic group from which he comes. While curriculum outlines and biblical materials from these courses may be helpful, their status structures and illustrations are not generally suitable.

Searching for material and critical evaluation of available materials is an important part of planning the Christian education program. The choice of materials, if possible, might be a joint decision by the teacher, the chaplain, and those on the therapy team of the institution.

The Bibliography contains some specific suggestions for curriculum in addition to basic books which will increase the teacher's ability to make judgments and choices.

General Objectives of Christian Education

It may seem strange to place the general objectives of Christian education toward the end of the chapter on curriculum. Objectives are usually stated first. Their placement here is easily explained. It is hoped that after the reader has considered some of the factors involved in curriculum for socially handicapped youngsters, he will study the traditional objectives and think of new interpretations and new experiences which might make them relevant to his group of youngsters. The traditional generalizations of the church have already failed the delinquent. The restatement here is for the teacher, not for the student. A new restatement of the significance of the faith for the troubled youngster must be made in the youngster's own language and in the life of the teacher, and this statement must be continually renewed with each growing experience. The objectives stated here are a guide by which the teacher may evaluate his work.

The following objectives were originally worked out by the Commission on General Christian Education of the National Council of Churches in 1958. In 1961 William C. Adamson, Director of the Child Study Treatment and Research Center of the Woods School, Langhorne, Pennsylvania, restated these objectives for persons working with exceptional children; they are presented here in Dr. Adamson's adaptation:

The supreme purpose of Christian education is:

» *to enable persons to become aware of the seeking love of God* as revealed in Jesus Christ, and

» *to respond in faith* to this love in ways that will help them:
   (1) to grow as children of God,
   (2) to live in accordance with the will of God, and
   (3) to sustain a vital relationship to the Christian community (and throughout God's world).

To achieve this purpose Christian education, under the guidance of the Holy Spirit, endeavors:

» *to assist persons, at each stage of development,*
   (1) to realize the highest potentialities of the self as divinely created,
   (2) to commit themselves to Christ, and
   (3) to grow toward maturity as Christian persons;

» *to help persons establish and maintain Christian relationships*
   (1) with their families,
   (2) with their churches, and
   (3) with other individuals and groups, (all) taking responsible roles in society, and (each) seeking in every human being an object of the love of God;

» *to aid persons in gaining a better understanding and awareness of*
   (1) the natural world as God's creation, and

(2) accepting the responsibility for conserving its values and

(3) using them in the service of God and of mankind;

» *to lead persons to an increasing understanding and an appreciation of the Bible, whereby*

(1) they may hear and obey the word of God; and

(2) to help them appreciate and use effectively other elements in the historic Christian heritage; and finally,

» *to enable persons to discover and fulfill responsible roles in the Christian fellowship* through faithful participation in the local and world mission of the church.[3]

CURRICULUM DECISION-MAKING

By now it must be obvious that planning curriculum involves making decisions. Some decisions must be made before the class meets: Who will teach the class? What time will it meet? How shall the youngsters be selected? What Christian education emphases seem most valuable for socially handicapped children? What characteristics of socially handicapped children seem to have relevance for a Christian education program?

After meeting with the class, there are decisions which the teacher must make: In what order should we consider the youngsters' religious questions? In which aspects of religion did the youngsters seem most interested? How should the group begin to discover answers to their questions? Would a filmstrip be useful? (Suggestions for teaching methods are given in chapter 7.)

During each class the teacher has decisions to make: Should I let Bill dominate the conversation right now? When should we get back to John's suggestion which was overlooked in the discussion? Are the youngsters getting too restless? How can I make Mary feel a part of the group? Every teacher carries on a dialogue with himself,

---

[3] Used by permission of Dr. Adamson.

deciding and redeciding, evaluating and questioning, anticipating and rebuking.

It is very important for these decisions to be made quickly and astutely and positively in teaching socially disturbed youngsters. This does not mean that the youngsters should not share in some of the decisions, but once the rules are decided upon, or directions given, the teacher must not waiver. Although defiant children may assault these decisions, the decisions must stand. These children need the security and the limitations on behavior which positive decisions represent.

Teaching is decision-making. The more stable the teacher and the greater his understanding of pupils and subject matter, the more competent he is to make the necessary decisions and stick to them. Good decisions made with insight make superior teaching. Poor decisions, and the resultant loss of a teaching opportunity, make for better decisions next time.

All teaching decisions do not need to be made in isolation. One of the advantages of including teaching assistants in the class program is the two-headed evaluation thus made possible. Where two or more teachers work together sympathetically and critically, everyone profits. Consultation with the institutional staff also will prove to be helpful in decision-making.

Evaluating Learning and Religious Growth

There are several levels on which a Christian education program for socially handicapped youngsters may be evaluated. Each is helpful in its own way. The kind of evaluation made will depend upon the objectives of the program. Testing the class knowledge of biblical content is not a valid test of a program aimed at developing within the individual a closer relationship with God. Biblical knowledge, however, is important in the teaching of a historical faith, provided this knowledge has meaning for present life. While the evaluative process is difficult, and often inadequate in sampling actual pupil growth, much can be learned from taking a critical look at what is happening in a Christian education program. As a result of evaluation helpful changes may be indicated in curriculum, in teaching procedures, or in other aspects of the program.

The following three levels of evaluation are suggested for the consideration of the teacher and chaplain.

Evaluation of intellectual knowledge. Do the youngsters know the significance of Jesus for the Christian faith? If they have been studying the parables of Jesus, do they know what a parable is? Do they know generally the content of the Bible? Informal evaluation of intellectual knowledge of the faith should be made before and after teaching. What the youngsters know upon joining a religious education class is significant for planning. What the youngsters have learned in the area of content is important as an evaluation of the teaching methods used and as a basis for future teaching.

A variety of tests of intellectual knowledge could be constructed. These might include class participation in the diagraming of the events of the life of Jesus, individual illustrations of parables or events in the life of Jesus, reviewing the list of questions originally asked by members of the class. Tests of intellectual knowledge do not need to take the usual form of true-false tests or filling in the blanks. Such tests are not especially exciting or challenging to youngsters who are chronic failures in school programs.

Evaluation of religious meanings. Evaluation in the area of religious meanings is more dependent upon the teacher's judgment. One teacher, after working with youngsters on a unit of study of personal relationships, asked these questions:

» Why do you think Jesus used only plural pronouns (we, ours, us) rather than singular pronouns (I, me, mine) in the Lord's Prayer?

» What is it supposed to mean in our actions to say we are all "children of our heavenly Father"?

Questions such as these might be included in group discussion or in personal talks with individuals rather than in a formal written test. Written tests often evaluate facility with the English language rather than personal understanding.

Another way of evaluating religious meanings is to suggest a series of problem situations in which youngsters in circumstances similar to those of persons in institutions were faced with important decisions. The class might consider together possible decisions and the decisions which most nearly represent a Christian point of view.

In the area of religious meanings, evaluation is a continuing process. It might be that the best time for evaluating the understanding of an individual youngster will be when chance remarks are made in the middle of class discussion. The teacher must be alert to these signs of new understanding. Creative ingenuity is certainly needed in this area.

Evaluation of change in individuals. The Christian faith itself gives us the basis for evaluating religious growth in persons. People who listened to Jesus and believed were changed. The astonishing statement of the impact of Peter and John upon those who observed their new lives in Christ is illustrative: "Now when they saw the boldness of Peter and John, and perceived that they were uneducated, common men, they wondered; and they recognized that they had been with Jesus" (Acts 4:13). Paul writes: "The works of the flesh are plain. . . . But the fruit of the Spirit is love, joy, peace, patience, kindness, goodness, faithfulness, gentleness, self-control" (Gal. 5:19, 22-23). While the teacher of rebellious youth may not expect to find "gentleness" as a result of Christian teaching, certainly an increasing manifestation of self-control on the part of an individual would indicate that values other than immediate self-satisfaction were influencing action.

A teacher's evaluation of change in students is necessarily subjective; however, when others working with the same individual sense a change in attitude or values it might be concluded that growth toward becoming a new person is taking place. As noted in chapter 5, none of us ever arrives at a state of perfection. Growth is slow and sin persists, yet each person has the potential for change and rebirth.

One chaplain describes an observation made by many workers with youth:

> It is important that we realize that children do not grow onward and upward to higher and higher spiritual or emotional maturity because we fill them hour by hour with "religious education." Children like adults have their "mountain-top experiences" and then fall in the valley. The "valley experiences" may be the time in the youngster's development when he is learning a great deal about himself and his God. During this period he may miss church, stop going to Sunday school, do poorly on a test, but he may also be growing. This is not necessarily a reflection on our teaching ability.[4]

---

[4] Chaplain Charles B. Grimm.

7 / Some Teaching Suggestions

"WHAT IS EDUCATION?" is a basic question that must be answered by every teacher. Is education the relaying of particular information from one person to another? Or is education the process by which persons are changed through new understandings which they have made their own? If a teacher believes that education is transmitting knowledge, then educational methods are primarily those of lecture, recitation, and memorization. If the teacher believes that education goes deeper, that it involves changes in persons, then other teaching methods must be added to the lecture, recitation, and memorization. The student must be personally involved in the educational process. It becomes important to know the individual children and to continually look for new ways to make knowledge meaningful to their lives.

Christian Education

Because the Christian faith is greater than rules and scriptural passages to be learned, Christian teachers need to think of education as more than passing on tradition. Paul wrote to the Corinthians: "And if I have prophetic powers, and understand all mysteries and all knowledge, and if I have all faith, so as to remove mountains, but have not love, I am nothing" (1 Cor. 13:2). Paul is saying that Christianity affects the inner self. What one is inside is important.

To become a Christian means to change. Being a Christian involves being a particular kind of person in particular kinds of relationships with other persons. Being a Christian means loving God as revealed in Jesus Christ. It is being a new creature. It is more than intellectual facts. Christian education is education toward salvation. This means that persons are changed through God's grace. (On pages 64-65 there is a list of objectives of Christian education based on a 1958 statement of the Commission on General Christian Education of the National Council of Churches.)

WHO ARE THE EDUCATORS?

Christian educators are Christians. This may seem to be a statement of the obvious; however, its implications are profound. It is through witnessing, believing Christians that the Christian faith is "caught" and understood. It is the community of persons who believe, who worship together, and who witness in their own particular ways, wherever they are, who are the real Christian educators.

Socially handicapped youngsters are particularly adept at spotting "phonies." They see much that is inconsistent between the words they hear about the church and the way in which the church exists as a community. Many of these children have never encountered an adult who really conveyed to them the love and the personal respect so characteristic of Jesus.

Socially handicapped youngsters know who really respects and cares about them although sometimes their suspicions and hostilities prevent them from meeting such persons. They know the teachers who live by their teachings. These youngsters need knowledge of the Christian faith, and they need this knowledge as it is lived by persons. In fact, because of their difficulties with formal education, they learn more quickly through example and experience with persons than they do through verbal lessons.

71

Further it should be noted that we, as teachers, are naïve when we feel that the lesson we have prepared to teach, or which we think we have taught, is exactly what is learned. Attitudes of the teacher and the other students, events preceding the class session, previous experiences with the church, different understandings of the meanings of words, as well as other factors prevent the student from even hearing what is actually being said. Many, many immeasurable factors contribute to the teaching process, in and out of the classroom. It is the whole environment—the whole Christian community of persons wherever they are encountered—that ultimately creates for children and youth the image of who a Christian is and an understanding of the Christian gospel.

You may wish to read again chapter 4—"The Teacher of the Socially Handicapped."

Some Bases for the Teacher's Planning

There are a number of factors in the lives of socially handicapped children and youth which should be recognized in connection with planning for teaching. The following factors seem to be particularly significant for Christian educators.

Previous school experiences. In chapter 3 it was noted that socially handicapped youngsters are often below the school grade for children of their chronological age. Sometimes this is because of limited intelligence; many times it is due to poor school experiences in the past. These children are often caught in a trap which begins with early school failure. This failure may be caused by any number of factors: illness, poor teaching, lack of readiness for school, parental disinterest, discrimination, emotional difficulties, hostility to adults, and many more subtle individual factors or combinations of factors. With early failure comes discouragement and a picture of the self as being incapable of dealing with prescribed learnings. Having started down this road of school failure, problems multiply; and unless the trend is reversed by very sensitive and sympathetic remedial teaching and guidance, the children will eventually drop out of school. These children never seem to develop a sense of the way to succeed within regularized school procedures. They are not "test-wise." Their intelligence is never made manifest in the school situation.

The ways these children learn are often not the ways of successful school students. Like all children they are continually learning at all times, in all places, but their learning style is different, and the contrast is most marked in the organized classroom. Thus it becomes extremely important to discover the ways in which the individual child does learn. Currently there is a great deal of research being carried out concerning the way people learn.

Ways of learning. Often socially handicapped youngsters are not wise in the use of *words*. Their verbal ability to express their feelings and experiences is limited. Many of these children have never had an adult with whom to talk about the things which really matter to them. Their real feelings are locked inside on a nonverbal level. Some of them are expert in the use of the language of the street but not of the schoolroom or the church. They know life as they experience it, but they are not able to say, "Because this is true, this also is . . ."

Words are basically symbols for meanings. It is possible that traditional Christian symbols might be used and Christian meanings developed for the youngsters. A potentially dangerous Christian symbol is that of three circles for the Trinity because of present commercial advertisements.

For the Christian teacher there seem to be three essential emphases:

1. For socially handicapped children and youth learning

is more meaningful in immediate person-to-person relationships in which there is mutual respect and acceptance. In this relationship there must be honesty about an individual's abilities and experiences and hope for growth. It is a relationship in which the child is not permitted to fail as a person but rather is helped to grow in an appreciation of the value of himself. This relationship does not impose as requirements of affection and acceptance the giving back of expected answers or the holding of "acceptable" life values. Love is not withheld because of rebellion or hostility on the part of the child. In effect the Christian teacher is teaching through living the Christian faith.

2. Concrete, immediate experiences are important in the education of socially handicapped youngsters. It means adapting for the classroom the methods by which the youngsters have learned effectively in the streets and in their gangs. It means using the teaching techniques proven to be effective with the slow learner. The teacher must use the life which the youngsters know as the basis of learning experiences. Religion needs to be seen as of practical value for right now.

One of the objectives of Christian education stated on page 64 is "to help persons establish and maintain Christian relationships with their churches." A lecture by the teacher about the church would not be the most effective way to build positive attitudes toward the church, nor should a discussion about the church by youngsters who may never have had significant experience with the church be considered completely satisfactory. Ideal teaching might involve experiences with the church both as it exists in a building in a nearby community or in the chapel of the institutional campus, and as it is manifested wherever persons meet together in the name of Christ. Some chaplains prefer to have the entire Christian education program and church services on the campus where the specific needs of the youngsters may be the primary consideration and where they are protected from being branded as "institution kids." Other chaplains see value for qualified youth in attendance at Sunday morning worship and evening youth groups in community churches which have been especially prepared to work with youth from the institution. They feel this experience for youngsters ready to accept its responsibilities helps to bridge the way back from the institution to the community. However church experiences are provided, they may become the basis of group study of the nature of the church, church ritual, and church history.

3. The active participation of students in the classroom situation is important. Many ways should be found for the students to use their hands and bodies in the process of learning. Puppet shows, map-making, role-playing, and the many other activities commonly found in church school programs are likely to be effective in teaching Christian education content, as well as in providing opportunities for group living as Christians. These methods require detailed advance planning so that the freedom of movement granted will not result in chaos. Class participation in advance planning is very helpful and should be followed by class evaluation of the group living as well as the product of the activity.

Individual differences. Educators today agree in principle, if not in practice, that all children are individuals. There are no two persons exactly alike. Each person has his own style of learning. Each person brings to the classroom a unique combination of past experiences and expectations. Each person needs to be recognized as a unique person. This is especially true of socially handicapped children and youth. As pointed out in chapter 6, religious education classes must be small enough so the needs and experiences of individuals can be expressed. There must be opportunity for informal talking and honest expression of the self with the teacher and with the others in the group. The larger the class, the less possibility there is to help a child "catch" the essence of being a Christian person. In a mass situation there is no opportunity for the real child to express his real feelings.

While it is not the responsibility of the Christian teacher to make a complete analysis of each child's problems or to attempt any kind of psychotherapy, it is important for the teacher to know the youngster's background, to listen to the youngster's expression of his present concerns, and to help him find the significance of religion in his life.

A variety of learning experiences should be planned which will provide an opportunity for individuals to use their own ways of learning and to discover ways of meeting their own needs. Occasionally the class might be divided into small work groups with a particular responsibility. On other occasions individual research might be encouraged. If institutional policy permits, small groups might be invited to participate in a special event or excursion outside of the regular class program.

Coordination with the institutional program. Any plan for teaching must be in harmony with the philosophy and the practice of the particular institution in which religious instruction classes are being held. The individual teacher is teaching on the invitation of the chaplain or those responsible for the religious program of the institution, and is subject to institutional regulations.

This does not mean, however, that the teacher may not try to explain possible changes in procedures which would facilitate a better educational program as he sees it. A request to those in authority for more or less time, for worship opportunities, or for a change in the size of classes would not be inappropriate.

Religious backgrounds. In planning teaching procedures, it is important to know the religious experience of the particular youngsters in a class. This information probably will not be available from the institution except for a statement of religious affiliation which may have been made upon entrance into the institution. A general view of the religious backgrounds and needs of socially handicapped children and youth is outlined in chapter 3, and it is noted that there is great variety among the youngsters. As a starting point with any group, it seems wise to assume (to yourself) religious illiteracy; or, at best, a limited knowledge of Bible stories and theological words such as "hell," "sin," and "saved," which may have little meaning for troubled lives. This does not mean, however, that the teacher would "talk down" to the student or act as if he were ignorant, but it does mean watching for clues which may indicate the extent of basic Christian understanding.

Experienced chaplains point out that teachers must be cautious of accepting at face value what seem to be sincere, significant religious questions asked by the youngsters. Some bright religious antagonists know they can keep a teacher occupied a whole session, or more, on a question such as "Why doesn't God answer prayer?" Actually the youngster may be only baiting the teacher and affirming the feeling that adults really do not know the "score." A limited consideration of questions asked early in the group's experience might be the best manner in which to deal with this situation. Youngsters might be encouraged to think further on the subject and bring in possible answers of their own. They might be helped to understand that there is no one answer to such questions and that each Christian must ultimately affirm answers of his own which seem most meaningful at a particular time in his life.

If an accepting environment has not already been created by previous teachers, it may take a teacher many months of living with boys or girls in a relationship where they feel free to reveal their real religious wonderings before change and growth toward religious maturity may begin to occur.

Currently public school educators, psychologists, and politicians are concerned with the education of socially handicapped youngsters in the public schools. Much money is being spent on research both by private foundations and by government. The following teaching suggestions reflect some of the opinions of persons experienced in this field. Wide reading of books in the Bibliography will supplement the following brief summary suggestions of ways of teaching.

Teaching through relationships. Be your real self. Establish in the first session the class routine and your expectations for student behavior. Rules once announced must be consistently enforced. Rules should be understood as necessary for group living and not as confinement of youngsters who are not to be trusted. Students should know the behavior expected of them and the routine of the class. A rule which requires one person to speak at a time, after being recognized by the teacher, is an elementary one to insist upon during discussions. Such a rule is basic to learning to respect other persons in the group. Further rules may be worked out as needed, and then enforced.

Provide all children with opportunities for growth. Do not be too quick to estimate which children are the natural leaders of the group, or which ones might cause trouble. Accept the contributions of all with appreciation and with the assumption that they are doing their best work. Should positive leadership emerge from within the group, this leadership should be channeled as a motivating force for new learning experiences.

Expect a period of time when the youngsters will test your knowledge and skill as a teacher. They may try all the tricks which they have learned through their many years of lack of conformity in schools. Once beyond this period of testing your personal integrity and consistency in discipline, they may begin to deal with matters they really care about.

Begin to structure your program to meet the specific needs of children as these needs appear. One child may seem to need an opportunity to do something he feels is important. Provide this opportunity for him by using one of his skills or by giving him a temporary major responsibility in a group project. Arranging chairs or being in charge of supplies might be helpful. Be sure to support the child in his efforts so that he does not fail. Subtle concern for individual feelings will contribute to growing relationships of trust and respect.

Teaching religious content. Use everyday language. Define and redefine, casually and formally, any religious words used. Do not assume that the youngsters' ideas about such basic concepts as God, prayer, or Jesus are adequate or even consistent with traditional theology. Street slang may be the extent of their education in religious vocabulary. Patience with this vocabulary is wise while attitudes and understandings are being dealt with.

Deal with everyday experiences. Pray with the youngsters informally during class. Talk about the problems which are on their minds at the moment—loss of privileges because of breaking institutional rules, worry about some member of a family, concern over a cottage friend who is having trouble, the meaning of authority. Through these conversations, religious ideas may be seen critically, and the meaning of religion in life may be evaluated in a way that has significance for present life. Further specific experiences are suggested in chapter 6.

Emphasize realistic heroes and heroines. The Bible heroes and the historical heroes of the church are persons who had hopes and problems and needed God's help. Happy endings, gentle goodness, and halos are not realistic to youngsters who have found life very difficult. For example, one current denominational curriculum, instead of emphasizing Joseph's greatness, emphasizes the problems which he faced as a person and the ways in which these problems were worked out with God. The youngsters will understand how the brothers of Joseph felt about Joseph's favored position with their father. One caution should be noted with regard to the Joseph story: youngsters who have many half brothers and sisters may be too close to the situation to be able to deal with it.

In all stories about heroes of the faith there should be an emphasis upon God's action and his grace so that children do not develop an idea that religion is the same thing as personal accomplishment. It is God who loves and extends his love and care to all persons.

Relate religious concepts to current life. Of course any printed curriculum must be adapted to individual class situations. This is particularly important for religious education classes in institutions for socially handicapped children and youth. As noted in chapter 6, the content of most denominational curriculum is middle class oriented with a great deal of emphasis upon verbal skills. These materials must be adapted and supplemented with illustrations and problems from the lives of youngsters living in an institution for delinquent children.

For example, a scripture passage commonly used in the older-elementary grades, "Be doers of the word and not hearers only," must be interpreted in light of the situation of socially troubled youngsters. They will need help in deciding upon small, realistic ways in which they can honestly begin to show concern for others. Denominational curriculum suggestions such as helping Mother when someone is sick are obviously not applicable.

ORGANIZING THE SESSION

Plan short units and complete sessions. It is important for the youngsters to feel the joy and success of accomplishment. Many cannot immediately accept long-term goals. Each session should seem worthwhile in itself. If possible it should have some practical meaning for their lives right then. Short-term goals and immediate rewards of affection and encouragement are extremely important for youngsters who have a history of failure and rejection.

Plan a variety of interrelated activities within one session. Movement from one activity or focus of attention to another will keep interest high and help to prevent the inattention which leads to discipline problems. Never plan for a teacher to talk for the whole class period. As an area of real interest develops in the classwork, the length of particular activities may be increased. Many youngsters who are slow to become interested in something outside of their present experience will work long and hard once their enthusiasm develops. As in all teaching, an occasional shift from quiet to active work is advantageous.

Use staff creatively. Time for religious instruction in institutions is limited. As noted, the class time may be more effectively used if there are co-teachers or assistants who may contribute particular teaching skills or who may be counted upon to give special attention to a few particular individuals during activity periods.

Include worship and music in a total Christian education program. Most institutions provide students with opportunities for worship either in a chapel or at local churches. If such experiences are not provided, the religious instruction period should include some informal worship and singing and occasionally a formal worship period.

Plan for relaxation and games in an extended program. If the religious instruction period extends toward an hour, some short fun experiences should be included. Games with factual religious content might be used. Games could include guessing biblical personalities, filling in the names of cities on a map of Palestine, or acting out historical events for another team to guess.

The following suggestions are a sample of the type of activity which is useful in teaching socially handicapped youngsters. Their use will depend upon the subject matter being taught, the educational skills of the particular group of youngsters, and the ages represented.

Having a discussion. Throughout this manual discussion has appeared as a primary way of working with youngsters. Such things as the elementary need of a plan for insuring the respect of the rights of others by speaking only one at a time have been pointed out. Group discussion requires very careful and subtle leadership. The leader is responsible for seeing that all who care to do so have an opportunity to speak, that the discussion remains with one aspect of the subject long enough to make possible depth consideration of the matter insofar as the group is able to do so, and that a feeling of acceptance pervades the group so that fear of expressing real feelings does not interfere. The leader's role is not to act as an authority, judging each contribution; but rather, it is to join in the search for meaning in the most helpful way, which might include offering needed factual information and expressing his own opinions when some kind of summary statement is needed.

Here is an outline of a discussion held by a chaplain in an institution for delinquent boys:

In the tenth meeting the boys began to ask some personal questions that were disturbing them. "Is there really a God?" asked Ted. Robert asked, "Where is God now?"

Ted was the one who put it on the level of honest feelings. "How do we know that somebody didn't make this stuff up?" he inquired. "Can you explain what you mean?" I asked Ted.

"Yeah, you know there's this church in Kansas City that asks people to give money. How do you know that they just don't make up this story about God to get your money?"

Later Ted was able to put his feelings into another kind of

make-believe story: "You know, a guy could have been sitting out under a tree one day, looked up around him, and saw what a mess the world was in and said, 'Someone must be able to straighten it out; I'll call him God.'" Ted came to the School to find some rhyme or reason for the chaos in his own world.

I realized that I could not answer the deeper questions that the boys were asking. I shared with them from my own experience and from the biblical writers who witnessed to their own struggles—but only when I was sure that the boys had reached their limit of personal involvement in the topic.[1]

Psychologists have learned a great deal about group-work methods. Within the institution there will be personnel who will be willing to give guidance in this area if requested to do so. A book listed in the Bibliography, *Learning Together in the Christian Fellowship* by Sara Little, will be helpful to the beginner.

Role-playing. Acting-out of life problems which are similar to those common to the class may serve as a basis for discussion of values and religious meanings. Role-playing, while an extremely useful learning activity, requires careful planning and skillful guidance. An inexperienced teacher would be wise to talk with an institutional staff person with regard to the use of role-playing, and to begin work initially with a very small group. The primary caution is that one must have control of the group, and a second caution is that one must avoid the danger of emphasizing the fun of acting rather than the meanings of the experiences involved. Putting oneself in another person's place and discovering new feelings is basic to role-playing.

Storytelling. Often children who have difficulty in school do not like to read. Storytelling by the teacher may create for them some of the excitement and the drama of biblical

---

[1] Smith, *op. cit.*

stories or current life situations which will motivate new interest in learning. Telling a story is superior to reading it, especially with these children. Good reading, however, is better than poor telling.

Making a time line. The physical activity of placing in relationship the historical events of the Hebrew-Christian tradition will help to establish their reality and historicity. If possible the time line should be a long-term project with historical events added as they are studied.

Making a map of Palestine.

Dramatizing biblical stories.

Using pictures. Pictures of Palestine will help to establish Jesus as a real person. It is important, however, to help the youngsters understand that we do not actually know what Jesus looked like. A collection might be made of portraits of Jesus, and time allowed for an expression of the students' feelings about them. The junior and junior high biblical curriculum pictures in denominational materials will be helpful.

Using filmstrips and movies. Good biblical audio-visuals which do not make Jesus look outdated or unmanly are very helpful in making the historical religion a firsthand experience. Modern-life pictures should be carefully previewed in terms of the backgrounds and hostilities of the children and youth.

Circulating religious books. A collection of appropriate religious books might be made available to the class. These books should be high in interest for youth, but should have a reading level of third or fourth grade. Books in an existing library should be carefully screened by a person familiar with religious literature for children. Books on biblical backgrounds, Bible stories, archeology, heroes of the faith, and religious questions would be appropriate. Also help-ful would be good fiction that is ethically and morally Christian although without specific Christian terminology. Some suggested pupils' books are included in the Bibliog-raphy.

Keeping up on current religious news. Older youth might enjoy establishing a bulletin board for newspaper clippings, or a file, if permanent facilities are not available. This ac-tivity would help the youth to appreciate the place of re-ligion in world affairs. Clippings might be collected on ecu-menical gatherings and such events as the establishment of a church center near the United Nations, as well as events and issues in current life which have ethical and moral implications.

Making Teaching Decisions

Ultimately it is the teacher in the classroom who makes the final decisions on session-by-session teaching proce-dures. No teacher finds this decision-making easy, and no teacher makes all the right decisions. The challenge, the joy, the excitement, and the rewards of teaching lie in com-ing to know a group of youngsters and creating with them situations in which they may change and grow to be new persons.

The teacher does not work alone. He works with God's present, living Spirit and with persons who share his vital concern. Each teaching experience is new and fresh for the teacher who tries to use creatively his own talents, the ma-terials available, and the resources latent within the young-sters. An illustration of such creative teaching is given on page 61.

8 / Relationships with Institutions for the Socially Handicapped

*

ONE OF THE VALUES of American schools and institutions is their diversity. We highly prize the right of the individual state and of the private corporation to fulfill their goals in their own way within the limits set by the people through legislative or executive action.

Institutions for socially handicapped children and youth reflect this diversity. Each institution has its own variations of philosophy, pattern of educational program, and therapy which reflect both the laws and regulations of the state in which it functions and the unique contributions of the personnel involved.

The variety of personnel on the staff of the institution is of particular significance to the religious educator. The total staff usually involves administrators, social workers, a consulting or resident psychiatrist, psychologists, house parents, teachers, maintenance employees, and others. The religious educator is part of the team. It is important that the religious educator be included in relevant staff meetings in order that his work is not done in isolation or in opposition to institutional policies and treatment plans.

The beginning Christian teacher may find that the knowledge and experience of the institutional staff is overwhelming, and at times might find that he has made teaching decisions which the staff does not think are the best. In such cases the teacher might remember that knowledge grows with experience, and that from controversial decisions comes greater understanding. Most professional workers in institutions would be the first to admit that there is a great deal yet unknown about how to help troubled children and youth.

The Christian teacher working in an institution where delinquent youngsters are under custody should be familiar with the particular institution in which he works. Several general statements can be made for the new teacher about his relationship to the institution:

The institution has the ultimate responsibility for the children and youth committed to it. The philosophy and rules of the institution must be known, accepted, and carried out in any work with youngsters under its jurisdiction.

The teacher must support the institution in all experiences with its students. While youngsters may be given the opportunity of "blowing off steam" to someone who is not directly responsible for their life in the institution, the institution should not be criticized by the teacher. A neutral position is best. This does not mean that the teacher should not listen sympathetically when youngsters complain, but that the teacher must not join in the complaints. For example, a girl may ask, "Don't you think a girl should go home when her mother is sick?" The social worker has probably already dealt with the matter. In the case of a serious problem, the teacher might speak quietly to the chaplain or supervisor of the religious education program. Direct breaking of confidences should be avoided.

The teacher needs to know the routine of the institution. One institution provides each teacher with a mimeographed sheet outlining in specific detail the procedures necessary for making the Christian education program run smoothly and in harmony with the total program. Such regulations as the following are mentioned:

All equipment needed for class (pencils, audio-visual equipment, and so on) should be requested a week in advance, of the administrative person on duty who will leave word so that this can be made available. It cannot be secured at the last minute.

Students are *not* to be excused to use the lavatory during class session. If it is necessary for a student to be excused he should be sent to the administrative staff member who will make necessary arrangements.

Dismissal. Sunday school starts at 1:45 and closes promptly at 2:45. There will be two bells at dismissal. First bell is a signal to close class and see that room is in order. Door should be kept closed until administrative staff member calls house groups for dismissal at second bell. Please do not allow students to remain after class for discussion as students should return to their cottages in a group and their housemother will be expecting them.

The Christian teacher is part of the total institutional staff. He needs to be familiar with the methods of therapy carried on with the youngsters. While the teacher is not a social caseworker, his conversations with youngsters are not in isolation from the total program of the institution. Communication should be maintained with members of the staff so that there is cooperation and mutual understanding of purpose. The teacher's personal relationships with individual institutional personnel should reflect the same Christian qualities as his relationships with students.

It is important for the Christian educator to recognize that his relationships with the man who cleans the classroom, the workman on the grounds, and the housemothers, as well as with the professional staff and the students should be at all times one of patience for the individual and appreciation of persons in Christian love. The teacher cannot expect to give children an understanding of Christian love if his love is extended only to those whom he wishes to impress.

Nonprofessional workers in the institution may be allies of the Christian teacher. Much of the youngsters' day is spent with them. In many institutions professional workers are not unaware of this relationship and consequently choose staff carefully and interpret for them the philosophy and therapy plans of the total program. The Christian teacher needs also to find ways of expressing to housemothers, guards, orderlies, and maintenance personnel the Christian understanding of the value of persons as "children of God" and to interpret for them the nature and purposes of the Christian education program. The chaplain and teacher may thus become known to the nonprofessional workers as persons to whom questioning youngsters could be referred. "Why don't you talk to the chaplain about that," might become a common suggestion.

The teacher never takes outside of the institution the confidential information gained about the persons with whom he is working. He does not mail letters for students or in any manner allow youngsters to use him as a way of breaking institutional regulations.

The teacher should take advantage of every opportunity to receive training from the institution in work with socially handicapped youngsters. If no formal training is available, individual staff members might be asked for guidance in the specific areas of group-work methods, understanding defiant behavior, or group discipline.

The same standards of conduct expected elsewhere on the institutional campus apply to the Christian education classroom. Courtesy should be demanded. If youngsters continue to disrupt the class, their behavior should be discussed with the appropriate staff member. The discipline of the group is ultimately the responsibility of the staff. If a teacher using acceptable classroom techniques is unable to control the behavior of an individual, that person is usually refused permission by the staff to attend class. Probably, if the teacher has retained a friendly attitude, the student will want to return to the class when he is given permission.

One chaplain has pointed out the unique place of the chaplain or Christian educator in the institution:

Although he represents the community of the faithful, his role is not clearly defined. The minister does not serve as a pseudomedical treatment specialist. His task is not medical, though it is therapeutic in that he is there to offer help. The representative of religion in an institution does not serve in a scientific context, but he does use the tools that science has discovered in order to understand human need and potential. The minister in the institution represents the concern of those who are outside the gates, the Christian community. He also symbolizes man's faith in God to work through the human spirit to transcend itself, to recreate itself, to heal itself. The Christian minister stands as the representative of the one who achieved perfect wholeness in life—Jesus the Christ.[1]

---

[1] Smith, *op. cit.*

Bibliography

THEOLOGICAL AND BIBLICAL BACKGROUNDS

BUBER, MARTIN. *I and Thou* (2d edition). Translated by Ronald Gregor Smith. Charles Scribner's Sons, 1958. A poetic description of the relation of person to person, person to things, and person to God. Requires several readings and is worth it. Much modern Christian thinking is based upon this book.

GRIMES, HOWARD. *The Church Redemptive*. Abingdon Press, 1958. A thoughtful consideration of the meaning of the church in our time with special consideration given to worship, Christian nurture, group life, and administration. Chapter 9, "The Outreach of the Fellowship," and chapter 10, "Providing Leadership for the Fellowship" are especially recommended.

HOWE, REUEL L. *Herein Is Love*. Judson Press, 1961. "A study of the biblical doctrine of love and its bearing on personality, parenthood, teaching, and all other human relationships." Written in a popular style.

_____. *Man's Need and God's Action*. Seabury Press, 1953. An exciting fresh discussion of the Christian faith in everyday life. Good reading; thought-provoking.

LOOMIS, EARL A., JR. *The Self in Pilgrimage*. Harper & Row, 1960. Gives theological and psychiatric insights into the lives of persons in their relationship to God.

PHILLIPS, J. B. *God Our Contemporary*. Macmillan Co., 1960. Deals simply and profoundly with the present spiritual poverty of society and the meaning of the Christian gospel for our time.

_____. *New Testament Christianity*. Macmillan Co., 1956. A presentation of the meanings of New Testament faith. The author is eminently qualified for writing for laymen.

_____. *The New Testament in Modern English*. Macmillan Co., 1958. A translation of the New Testament into modern English which gives the reader greater understanding of the meaning of the Bible for our time.

ROBERTS, DAVID E. *Psychotherapy and a Christian View of Man*. Charles Scribner's Sons, 1950. An important analysis of current religious thinking in light of the experience of psychotherapists. Recommended for careful study. Popularly written.

SHERRILL, LEWIS JOSEPH. *The Gift of Power*. Macmillan Co., 1955. Deals with God's gift of power to the self and the Christian community in these times of change and anxiety. Practically related to the ministry of Christian education.

STINNETTE, CHARLES R., JR. *Faith, Freedom, and Selfhood*. Seabury Press, 1959. A study of the meaning of freedom for the self and the Christian, written by a psychiatrist. Very stimulating.

TEMPLE, WILLIAM. *Christianity and Social Order*. London: Student Christian Movement Press, 1950. A short study by an eminent British theologian of the relationship of religion and the church to economic, political, and social problems.

THIELICKE, HELMUT. *Christ and the Meaning of Life*. Edited and translated by John W. Doberstein. Harper & Row, 1962. A book of sermons and meditations which are vivid expressions of Christian meaning for a modern world, by an eminent German preacher and theologian. Covers the time from World War II to space exploration.

_____. *The Silence of God*. Wm. B. Eerdmans Publishing Co., 1962. A series of dynamic sermons which express the vital nature of Christianity in a world grappling with the issues of existence. Preached in Germany between 1942 and 1951.

UNDERSTANDING OUR PUPILS

ALEXANDER, FRANZ, and HEALY, WILLIAM. *Roots of Crime*. Alfred A. Knopf, 1935. Points out the complexity of the roots of crime and the significance of the combination of factors within the individual personality. Psychoanalytic case studies are used for this purpose.

BENNETT, IVY, *Delinquent and Neurotic Children*. Basic Books, 1960. Contains an excellent description of the needs and problems of the delinquent child and youth.

BRITT, STEUART HENDERSON. *Social Psychology of Modern Life* (revised edition). Holt, Rinehart & Winston, 1949. An enduring text on social psychology. Chapter 21, "Delinquency Patterns," is particularly recommended. This chapter deals with attempts at treating problems of delinquency and crime.

BUTCHER, RUTH L., and ROBINSON, MARION O. *The Unmarried Mother*. Public Affairs Pamphlet No. 282. Public Affairs Committee (22 East 38th Street, New York, N. Y. 10016), 1959. 25 cents. A very practical description of the backgrounds, problems, needs, and possible actions of the girl or woman who bears a child out of marriage. Recommended for all teachers of delinquent girls.

CONANT, JAMES BRYANT. *Slums and Suburbs*. McGraw-Hill Book Co., 1961. A controversial book which raises questions and makes observations about education and its relation to sociological factors of our time.

GOODMAN, PAUL. *Growing Up Absurd*. Random House, 1956. A serious, thorough, and honest evaluation of youth and the world in which they are growing up. The problems and situations described are those which have affected most institutionalized youth.

HILTNER, SEWARD. *Sex and the Christian Life*. A Reflection Book. Association Press, 1957. A short, practical consideration of sex in relation to biblical teaching, church history, and modern thought. Helpful background for a teacher of youth.

KVARACEUS, WILLIAM C., and MILLER, WALTER B. *Delinquent Behavior: Culture and the Individual*. National Education Association, 1959. A significant treatment of the factors involved in delinquency, written by persons with wide experience in this field.

MYERS, CHAUNCIE KILMER. *Light the Dark Streets*. Dolphin Books. Doubleday & Co., 1957. The story of an Episcopalian vicar who worked with a gang on the Lower East Side of Manhattan. Exciting, and revealing of the tremendous problems involved.

REDL, FRITZ, and WINEMAN, DAVID. *Children Who Hate*. Collier Books. Free Press of Glencoe, 1951. A description of experiences with socially disturbed children in a residential therapy situation. Extremely valuable reading for the teacher of delinquents.

RIESSMAN, FRANK. *The Culturally Deprived Child.* Harper & Row, 1962. An excellent, easily read analysis of the child who is often found in the institution for the socially handicapped. Particular emphasis is placed on the relationship of the deprived child and the schools.

SALISBURY, HARRISON E. *The Shook-up Generation.* Harper & Row, 1958. Brings a teacher up to date on the language and the life of inner city youth gangs.

YOUNG, LEONTINE R. *Out of Wedlock.* McGraw-Hill Book Co., 1954. A study of the problems of the unmarried mother and her child. Many helpful case illustrations are given.

FOR THE TEACHER

Helping Teachers Understand Children. American Council on Education, 1945. A classic book which uses actual teaching experiences in the schools to help the reader gain a better understanding of the teacher and the child working together.

JERSILD, ARTHUR J. *When Teachers Face Themselves.* Bureau of Publications, Teachers College, Columbia University, 1955. An excellent, easy-to-read book intended to help teachers understand themselves and develop healthy attitudes toward teaching.

MACKIE, ROMAINE P.; KVARACEUS, WILLIAM C.; and WILLIAMS, HAROLD M. *Teachers of Children Who Are Socially and Emotionally Maladjusted.* U.S. Department of Health, Education, and Welfare. Office of Education, Bulletin No. 11, 1957. Available from U.S. Government Printing Office, Washington. 45 cents. Very helpful in pointing out the kind of teacher needed.

PALMER, CHARLES E. *The Church and the Exceptional Person.* Abingdon Press, 1961. Contains a survey of the characteristics and needs of many kinds of exceptional persons and suggests ways in which the church might minister to them.

PASSOW, A. HARRY (ed.). *Education in Depressed Areas.* Bureau of Publications, Teachers College, Columbia University, 1963. Contains a review of the current thinking by school educators about the problems and the potentialities of urban children and youth. Many practical teaching suggestions are made.

POWDERMAKER, HORTENSE. *Probing Our Prejudices.* A unit for high school students. Harper & Row, 1944. An old book which contains many valuable suggestions for the teacher about working with prejudices.

REDL, FRITZ, and WATTENBERG, WILLIAM W. *Mental Hygiene in Teaching* (2d edition). Harcourt, Brace & World, 1959. An excellent basic text written by psychologists with wide experience with children who have conflicts and hatreds. Contains a helpful appendix with definitions of special psychological terms.

TECHNIQUES

BARNLUND, DEAN C., and HAIMAN, FRANKLYN S. *The Dynamics of Discussion.* Houghton Mifflin Co., 1960. An excellent depth study of the process of group discussion.

FRANK, JEROME D. *Group Methods in Therapy.* Public Affairs Pamphlet No. 284. Public Affairs Committee (22 East 38th Street, New York, N. Y. 10016), 1959. 25 cents. A brief, but comprehensive, presentation of various group methods of therapy, their values, and limitations. Recommended as part of the library of the beginning worker with youth under custody.

HILTNER, SEWARD. *The Counselor in Counseling.* Abingdon Press, 1952. Written for the person beginning as a counselor. Easily read, with ample case illustrations.

HOWE, REUEL L. *The Miracle of Dialogue.* Seabury Press, 1963. An excellent, readable, consideration of dialogue as the principle of effective communication between persons.

LINK, HELEN K. *Our Place in God's Plan* (curriculum for older elementary children). Greater Philadelphia Council of Churches (1421 Arch St., Philadelphia, Pa. 19102). $4.50 plus postage. Contains materials worked out at the Youth Study Center in Philadelphia. A twelve-unit course for children in custody.

LITTLE, SARA. *Learning Together in the Christian Fellowship.* John Knox Press, 1956. A description of the Christian learning, changing, and growing that may take place in a group study.

MAY, ROLLO. *The Art of Counseling*. Abingdon Press, 1939. An older book written for pastors, teachers, and workers in the church.

NICHOLS, HILDRED, and WILLIAMS, LOIS. *Learning About Role-Playing for Children and Teachers*. Association for Childhood Education International (3615 Wisconsin Avenue, N.W., Washington, D. C. 20016), 1960. 75 cents. A "how to" bulletin which contains principles and illustrations of role-playing with younger children.

WITTENBERG, RUDOLPH M. *The Art of Group Discipline*. Association Press, 1951. A short, practical consideration of the meaning and process of discipline within a group.

FOR THE PUPIL

DUVALL, EVELYN MILLIS, and HILL, REUBEN. *When You Marry* (revised edition). Association Press, 1962. Deals with wedding plans, physiology, and family life. Middle class oriented.

HARNER, NEVIN C. *About Myself*. United Church Press (The Christian Education Press), 1950. A popular book for older youth; useful in helping youth to understand themselves in relation to the faith. Written for middle-class youngsters.

_____. *I Believe*. United Church Press (The Christian Education Press), 1950. A helpful presentation to youth of the Christian faith. Might be read by good high school senior or used in group study.

KUNKEL, FRITZ. *My Dear Ego*. United Church Press (The Pilgrim Press), 1947. A guide to help older youth understand themselves as growing persons in control of their decision-making. Middle-class without orientation toward severe personal disturbances.

MARAMARCO, PHYLLIS. *Prayers for Girls at Long Lane School*. Connecticut Council of Churches, 1961. Simple, profound prayers based on the thoughts of girls in custody. Excellent.

WALPOLE, ELLEN WALES. *Why Should I?* Harper & Row, 1949. Asks basic questions about life and Christianity, and suggests ways of thinking about answers. Should be helpful.